D1526758

Intertwined
With
Jesus

Beverly Beeghly Avers

Beverly Beeghly Avers

Fairway Press
Lima, Ohio

Intertwined With Jesus

Library of Congress Control Number: 2019904576

Artist: Kim Lattimer Reeder, Front Cover

ISBN-13: 978-0-7880-4085-6
ISBN-10: 0-7880-4085-5   PRINTED IN USA

For: My children:

Kathleen Louise Moore, Diane Marie and husband Tod
William Linton.

Grandchildren:
Caitlin Diane and Kristin Erica Saupe, Sean Patrick and
Lindsay Grace Moore

In Memory of:
Christine Glenna Avers

I give God the Glory and Praise for the creation of this
book.
I thank you for reading this book and pray that you
know that you are intertwined with Jesus as God's
beloved child.
Beverly

Acknowledgments

I wish to thank Doctor Reverend Diann O'Bryant for editing the book and giving her suggestions. I thank Barbara Davids, Kim LaRue, and Diane Linton for reading the book and giving their suggestions. I am thankful to Carrie Hover for meeting with me and helping with the suicide chapter. For support, I thank my family, Upper Room women at Powell United Methodist Church, and Villas of Riverbend Bible study ladies. I thank Nancy Johnston and her grandson, Cole Linville, for sharing their God wink story. I am thankful for Kim Lattimer Reeder for her artistic ability with the cover of the book.

Contents

Introduction

A revelation, a God wink moment came upon me July 7, 2017, as I read my Upper Room devotion book - John 15:5: "I am the vine you are the branches." The writer of the devotion said that "One day I stopped to look more closely at one of these trees and its large entangled roots." The roots as I read it became *intertwined* and I said, Oh, my, *intertwined with Jesus*. My published book I*ntertwined - Beverly and Barbara in the Womb*, came to mind. Oh, my Lord, *intertwined with Jesus* are you asking me to write another book at this time, titled *Intertwined with Jesus*? Oh, this is too overwhelming for me to grasp, You will have to teach me what this means! I need to be still, to research and discover the meaning. Then I will write another book if this is your will for me to do so.

It is overwhelming, being *intertwined with Jesus* and being connected always. John Wesley challenges us to work toward perfection, toward sanctification and this little book will help us toward this goal.

A friend of mine, Roselee, said she felt relieved when she read in her Upper Room devotion that others were having trouble staying connected with Jesus, that we have chores to do and that is ok, that is all part of life. Brother Lawrence has helped us to see that doing dishes can be part of our life with Christ.

Do not be discouraged, keep looking to Jesus remembering that you are intertwined with Jesus and nothing can separate you from Him. Praise God!

Scripture is taken from the New Revised Standard Version of the Bible unless noted otherwise.

One of the chapters is on suicide. I have included it because it is becoming so tragic and concerning with our youth. We need to address suicide prevention, be more aware, and sense when we see a concern and reach out to help the person in need. It is so hidden as we wear our masks of deception. May the Lord guide us in love.

Thank you for reading *Intertwined with Jesus*. May you know that *you* are *intertwined with Jesus*; say it often to stay connected, to fight off the evil one, and be victorious.

God bless,

Beverly

Chapter 1

Meaning of Intertwined

Come with me and let's define *intertwined*. I looked in Webster's Dictionary, and the dictionary on the internet and it gave the meaning as: "to twist or braid together, to interweave with one another. Twisted: to entwine two or more threads as to produce a single strand; to wind or coil vines, ropes, to interlock or interface, to turn or open." The internet: meaning: "twist or twine together, interweave, braid, splice, knit, weave, mesh, difficult to separate, united. If two or more things are intertwined they are closely connected."

Sarah Young in *Jesus Calling* December 30, uses *intertwined*: "Marvel at the beauty of a life *intertwined* with My presence." On October 23, she wrote, "As you are increasingly filled with *My being*, you experience joyous union with *Me*: I in you and you in Me. Your *Joy-In-Me* and my *Joy-In-you* become "intertwined" and inseparable."

Being *intertwined with Jesus* is being connected, united, one, interwoven, like a braided, twisted, buttered pretzel. At first, I wanted to locate a place in my body, like my heart, where Jesus enters, then I realized Jesus is in my entire being, bringing oneness.

Let us pray: O Lord you are right here present within me, *intertwined* never to leave me. Help me this day to remember you are with me, helping and guiding me, understanding, forgiving and loving me making all things possible through Christ. Praise you O Lord. Amen.

"I pray that, according to the riches of his glory, he may grant that you may be strengthened in your inner being with power through his Spirit, and that Christ may dwell in your hearts through faith, as you are being rooted and grounded in love" (Ephesians 3:16-17).

Chapter 2

(John 15: 1, 4-5),
Vine and the Branches

"I am the Real Vine and my Father is the Farmer. Live in me. Make your home in me just as I do in you. In the same way that a branch can't bear grapes by itself but only by being joined to the vine, you can't bear fruit unless you are joined with me. I am the Vine, you are the branches. When you're joined with me and I with you, the relation intimate and organic, the harvest is sure to be abundant. Separated, you can't produce a thing.... But if you make yourselves at home with me and my words are at home in you, you can be sure that whatever you ask will be listened to and acted upon" (See: The Message).

Let's put on our gloves now, get your shovel, feel the dirt, for we are going to get grounded, rooted in the Lord and see how we are *intertwined with Jesus*.

Christ is the vine, God is the vine-grower caring for the branches. The branches are all of us who claim to be followers of Jesus Christ. Our first step is to be ourselves before God - to repent, which is "to cease play-acting and throw ourselves on the mercy of God relying on Christ's forgiveness, grace, mercy and love." We ask Jesus to come into our lives, and forgive our sins.

Jesus was crucified for us while we were still sinners. Picture all your sins on that cross - past, present, and future, on the cross of Jesus. Invite Jesus to "come, come Lord Jesus, come; come in today, come in to stay, come into my heart, my whole being today," and Jesus comes.

As you confess your sins you are forgiven. Now your sins are gone, "as far as the east is from the west," never to be brought up again (Psalm 103:12).

May you remember your baptism for the water (whether immersed or sprinkled) flowed over your being as the Spirit of God entered. Remember you belong to Christ, feel the water washing over you, cleansing you of all your sins, making you Christ's own, sealing you with Christ's mark of ownership. For you are *intertwined with Jesus.* You say it, (your name) _____*is intertwined with Jesus.* (If you have not been baptized, please speak with a pastor).

In three days Jesus arose. Christ is alive and lives in us. Christ has given us Himself, enabling us to be with Him forever. Believers of Jesus are promised eternal life (John 3:16), "For God so loved the world that God gave his only Son, so that everyone who believes in Him may not perish but may have eternal life." For we shall dwell in the house, God's home, in God's presence forever (Psalm 23:6). God's word contains God's promises.

Jesus then told his disciples and us that: "I will ask the Father and He will give you another advocate, counselor, to be with you forever. You will know Him because He abides in you. I will not leave you orphaned; I am coming to you. Those who love me will keep my word and we will come to them and make our home with them" (John 14:16, 23). "We know that we abide in Him and He in us because He has given us his Spirit" (1 John 4:13).

"Abiding in Christ means resting in Christ Jesus and letting Christ do the work." Andrew Murray in his book, *The True Vine* continues to say, "we have placed the emphasis on abiding as work we have to do instead of the living Christ, in whom we were to be kept abiding, who

Himself was to hold and keep us. We thought of abiding as a continual strain and effort and we forget that it means to *rest* from effort to one who has found the place of abode (home)."

(Pause - Stop And Read Again)

Amazingly, we are to rest in Jesus and let Jesus do our work. It's time to let go of all that stifles, all that hinders, to throw off all that enslaves us so we can give all to Jesus. Jesus is embracing you. He has his arms around you, you belong to Jesus. Surrender all and feel Jesus loving you. Now praise the Lord for God's forgiveness, grace, mercy and love.

Let us Pray: O Lord, you are the vine, I am the branch, I am part of you, attached, intertwined. I believe in You as my personal Savior. I come asking forgiveness for: _____. Help me release these sins and distractions to you for they are gone, gone as far as the east is from the west never to be brought up again. Thank you dear Jesus for the cross, for dying for me. I don't deserve this but this is your grace, your mercy given for me. O Lord, help me to stop and slow down and realize that I am "abiding in You," I am *intertwined with Jesus*. As I abide in You I give all my control issues to You. Help me to depend on your gentle whisper to guide, direct, and then to rest in the assurance that you are all I need. In Jesus' Name I pray. Amen.

Remember: "In the Name of Jesus Christ you are forgiven"!

Chapter 3

Daily Appointment Time With God

What a privilege to meet with our Lord each day. It doesn't matter what time, or where, just set a time and place and do it. No guilt trips or pressure intended, it is an important date to keep. But you say, "I have two jobs, three kids, a husband and two dogs. When?" Ask our Lord, how and when. It could be on a lunch break, or another break. Then just invite the Lord to come and enfold you in God's love and rest. Open your Bible and get fed.

I have an appointment with God every morning at 9:00. It is a special time and I am excited to get to my favorite chair. I have my favorite study guides and devotionals like: *The Bible, Upper Room, My Utmost for His Highest, Jesus Calling, Jesus Lives, Daily Strength from WEEC,* and the Bible study that I am currently in. To begin reading the Bible, Joni and Friends has the Chronological Bible Study for a Year. Or start reading the "Bible through in One Year" guides you through the study of God's Word. There are many study guides so I don't have to give you detailed ways to prepare your appointment time. I encourage you to join a support group at church whether as a couple or single. It is powerful to be in a confidential group where you study, pray and share your concerns with others. Take a tour of your Christian bookstore and choose a Bible study.

Begin: We just learned we are to rest in Jesus. I suggest that you begin with prayer asking Jesus to come, picturing being *intertwined with Jesus*: being embraced, held, and loved. Tell Jesus what is on your heart, mind, and what you need this day giving it all to Jesus. Then read the devotionals, and Bible and pray for others from your prayer request list. Beth Moore in her book, *The Beloved Disciple* says, "to begin your prayer with 'I know you always hear me,' and conclude 'Father, I thank you that you have heard me.' "Practice God's presence and pray as if He's really listening because God is."

Henri Nouwen says, "Prayer is the discipline of listening to that voice of love. Jesus spent many nights in prayer listening to the voice that had spoken to him at the Jordan River. We too must pray. Without prayer, we become deaf to the voice of love and become confused by the many competing voices asking for our attention. Prayer is other than meditation, it develops the life of God in us."

Jesus said to his disciples, "Sit here, watch, and pray." Nouwen says, "If they had been like some of us they would have said, 'No, it is absurd. We must go and do something.' If we do not watch and pray we shall be led into temptation before we know where we are. Watch and pray lest you enter into temptation."

Harry Emerson Fosdick says, "Prayer is neither chiefly begging for things, nor is it merely self-communion; it is that loftiest experience within the reach of any soul, communion with God."

Oswald Chambers, "If You Will Ask" says that "prayer for Jesus is not a way to get things from God, but so that we may get to know God.... The purpose of prayer is to reveal the presence of God, equally present at all time and in every condition."

Gerald G. May in his book, *The Awakened Heart* says, "Breath is the most common symbol of the spirit, and it is always with us as a reminder of our presence in love. Breath is also used as an aid to heart prayer." May says,

"Keep your time simple: Take a breath, ask the Holy Spirit to come and open your mind to understand and direct, then breathe in, and say – 'come Lord Jesus, come, and breath out and say – 'have mercy on me. Amen'. Then relax and be still and know that I am God."

And you can do your breath prayer breathing in *intertwined with Jesus*, and breathing out: "have mercy on me", or whatever words you would like to use.

Let us pray: Come Lord Jesus come, for I know you always hear me for you are right here *intertwined* with me. I pray that you will help me keep focused on you this day, and on the power of your Spirit to discern, direct, understand and obey. Help me surrender in complete devotion giving you my gratitude for all you have done and are doing for me. O Lord, may your grace and peace be in me and upon me.

Now let us do our breath prayer: breathe in, and say: "come Lord Jesus, come" breathe out: "have mercy on me." Do it again: breathe in, and say: "I'm *intertwined with Jesus*", breathe out - "have mercy on me." Then relax and be still and know that I am God. Father, I thank you that you have heard me. In Jesus Name I pray. Amen.

Chapter 4

First and Greatest Commandment

Jesus was asked which commandment in the law is the greatest. And he said, "You shall love the Lord your God with all our heart, with all our soul, and with all your mind"(Matthew 22:36-37). For "the chief end and duty of man is to love God and to enjoy him forever." (Westminster Cathechism)

Picture the Lord Jesus coming into your whole being, your body. "Do you not know that your bodies are members of Christ?"(1 Corinthians 6:15). "Or do you not know that your body is a temple of the Holy Spirit within you?" (1 Corinthians 6:19).

Nouwen says, "The *heart* is that place where body, soul, and spirit come together as one. It is the seat of the will. The heart is the central unifying organ of our personal life. The heart determines our personality, a place where God dwells." He continues to state that, "Our heart-the center of our being – is a part of God. It is that sacred space within us where God dwells and we are invited to dwell with God."

Rebecca Lair and Michael J. Christensen in their book, *The Heart of Henri Nouwen* said, "It was Nouwen's deep conviction that every human being is born in intimate communion with the God who created us in love. We belong to God from the moment of our conception. Our heart is that divine gift which allows us to trust not just God but also our parents, our family, ourselves, and our world."

Picture Jesus touching your mind and body. "Present your bodies as a living sacrifice holy and acceptable to God which is your spiritual worship. Do not conform to the world but be transformed by the renewing of your *minds* so that you might discern what is the will of God" (Romans 12:1-2).

We are to love the Lord with all our *soul*. Thomas Kelly gave this excellent description of the soul by Meister Eckhart: "Deep within us all there is an amazing inner sanctuary of the soul, a holy place, a Divine center, a speaking voice, to which we may continuously return. Eternity is at our hearts, pressing upon our time-torn lives, warming us with intimations of an astounding destiny, calling us home to itself. It is a dynamic center, a creative Life that presses to birth within us. And He is within us all."

Thomas Moore in his book, *Care of the Soul* said the first point to make about the care of the *soul* is that it is not primarily a method of problem solving. Its goal is not to make life problem-free but to give ordinary life the depth and value that come with soulfulness. Soul is not a thing but a quality or a dimension of experiencing life and ourselves. It has to do with depth, value, relatedness, heart, and personal substance."

"Get to the soul" was the Lord's message when I asked God about taking the position of working with special needs children. My first job was working as a home-based specialist. I would go to the children's homes and do activities. One of my first visits was with a severely mentally challenged child. That day I found myself on the floor, beside her, in the living room reading a book. To my sheer amazement I got lost in time and space for I was so connected with her soul. I have never forgotten that special moment with this special child. I had touched her soul for there was nowhere else to go and she had touched mine. I had received a glimpse of being *intertwined with Jesus*, not knowing it. Nouwen says, "Handicapped people who have such a limited ability to learn, can let their heart speak easily and thus reveal a mystical life that for many intelligent people seems unreachable."

In the inner most part of my being (soul), I am *intertwined with Jesus*, it is a sacred place in faith. I can go there, *intertwined with Jesus* like I was in the womb with my twin sister, Barbara. We were *intertwined*, touching, playing, present. Jesus is ever present wanting our affection, our acknowledgement. We can go there, right within our being and He is there welcoming us. "Oh my Lord, I cry, help me with whatever I need, and I find you there."

Let us pray: Come Holy Spirit help me, _____ (your name), to love you with all my heart, soul, and mind. I can't do this alone, I need your help to love you. You are so present, yet I am so distant, help me love in a way I can't imagine. Touch my heart and soul where you know it needs your help. Touch my mind as it plays all kinds of games taking me places that I don't understand; bring me back to you. Thank you Father, Son, and Holy Spirit. In Jesus' Name I pray. Amen.

Chapter 5

Falling "In" Love

Again, I am in awe. Why do we make our journey so difficult thinking it is so hard to follow when all we have to do is *let go* and let our Lord Jesus take over? We get all caught up in how we can do what we think is required and discover Jesus is here, right here within, *intertwined* and all we have to do is *let go and let Jesus.* We are to fall in love with Jesus and allow Jesus to take control of our lives. Jesus calls us His friends. Individually, we are attached to Him as a branch; as the branch is dependent upon the vine for all things. Jesus tells us: I am here to provide, supply, and be for you all that you require. Why are we so stubborn? So stiff-necked, so strong willed, so prideful? We love falling in love, desiring love, and love is here, within us, just ready for our obedience of dependency. But that's it, we don't want to be dependent on anyone. We tell our friends, "No, I can do it, I don't need you to help me with my studies, transport me, or *you fill in the blank.*"

Jesus is right here with us, in us to help us, yet we by-pass him for our own way of doing our thing. We need to know and remember that we have received Jesus' divine nature and all his characteristics are in us, calling us to yield ourselves to conformity to Jesus. As we yield in dependency on Jesus for strength we then have no cares for Jesus Christ provides all we need. For "I can do all things through Christ who strengthens me" (Philippians 4:13).

Andrew Murray says: As we abide in Christ Jesus, we realize it "comes to be nothing more nor less than the restful surrender of the soul to let Christ have all and work all, as completely as in nature the branch knows and seeks nothing but the vine."

Jesus sent us the Holy Spirit to help us surrender and give our love and dependency on Jesus for we cannot do this alone. Murray continues to tell us to take notice that Christ said, "Abide in me; I am the vine that brings forth, and holds and strengthens and makes fruitful the branches. Abide in me, rest in me, and let me do my work. Let each day, in our quiet time, in the inner chamber with Him and his Word, our chief thought and aim be to get the heart fixed on him, in the assurance: all that a vine ever can do for its branches, my Lord Jesus will do, is doing, for me. Give Him time, give Him your ear, that He may whisper and explain the divine secret: 'I am the Vine.'"

Let us pray: Oh Lord, you are the Vine, I am your branch completely dependent and abiding in You. I come to You loving Father, and I know by asking, You will give me what I ask according to your Word. Empower me through your Holy Spirit to be all that You want me to be as I reach out to others in Your love. May You receive all the Glory. In Jesus' Game I pray. Amen.

Chapter 6

Worship

"Make a joyful noise to the Lord, all the earth. Worship the Lord with gladness; come into his presence with singing. Know that the Lord is God. It is he that made us and we are his; we are his people, and the sheep of his pasture. Enter his gates with thanksgiving and his courts with praise. Give thanks to him, bless his name. For the Lord is good; his steadfast love endures forever, and his faithfulness to all generation" (Psalm 100).

As Pastor Bev, oh how I enjoyed going to the church I was serving and opening the doors of the church getting ready for worship. What a privilege to open wide the doors for all to come and lift up their praises in song and love, to hear God's message.

White states that Paul W. Hoon from his book: *"The Integrity of Worship*, defines Christian worship as God's revelation of himself in Jesus Christ and man's response…. Through his word, God discloses and communicates his very being to man…. It is a reciprocal relationship. God takes the initiative in addressing us through Jesus Christ and we respond through Jesus Christ using a variety of emotions, words and actions."

In Roman Catholic circles, James White says, "It has been common to describe worship as "the glorification of God and the sanctification of humanity… The church, (*ekklesia*) are those called out from the world… We assemble to meet God and encounter our neighbors."

Come and worship our Lord, sing God's praises, release your fears, let go of all the baggage of resentment, misunderstandings, and sins. Just feel those hurts and wounds released, the daggers of words misspoken healed with God's salve of forgiveness. Remember what the Lord Jesus Christ has done for you and be thankful. Alleluia, praise the Lord. We are here to give God the glory, the honor, and the praise; to be filled with the overflowing power of the Holy Spirit and love of God that brings joy to our soul! We are *intertwined with Jesus.* Can you just imagine how happy Jesus is to be in the sanctuary of God with you!

We come to worship to receive communion, the eucharist (Thanksgiving), the sacrament (the visible form of an invisible grace) of our Lord. Eucharist is a Greek word, *charis,* which means gift or grace. Nouwen says, "What else is the eucharistic life but a life of gratitude."

However you believe, come and receive this sacrament to remember our Lord and become empowered to be God's beloved child. And be thankful for God's way of making this possible through Jesus Christ's body and blood given for you and me. Can you imagine how thrilled Jesus is to give you himself this day? Ponder and give Jesus your praise and thankfulness.

"Hallelujah! Praise God in his holy house of worship, praise him under the open skies. Praise him for his acts of power, praise him for his magnificent greatness; Praise with a blast on the trumpet, praise by strumming soft strings; Praise him with castanets and dance, praise him with banjo and flute; Praise him with cymbals and a big bass drum, praise him with fiddles and mandolin. Let every living, breathing creature praise God! Hallelujah!"(Psalm 150 - The Message).

"Do you want the presence of God to be revealed in your life in a powerful way? Worship him from your heart. Read your Bible with a passion for his fellowship.

Sing your congregational songs while meditating on each word. Fellowship with other believers with a thankfulness for the Spirit that works in and through them. As Paul instructs, "Sing psalms, hymns and spiritual songs with gratitude in your hearts to God" (Colossians 3:16). The warm, welcoming presence of God will be as real as the praises of your heart. (Daily Strength)

"Praise the Lord! Praise God in his sanctuary: praise him in his mighty firmament! Praise him according to his surpassing greatness! Let everything that breathes praise the Lord!"(Psalm 150:1-2, 6).

Define worship for you. Allow the Holy Spirit to spring forth in you and express your gratitude and praise for the privilege of worshipping our Lord.

Let us pray: (pray your prayer---------) and then close with the Lord's Prayer: "Our Father who art in heaven, hallowed be thy name. Thy kingdom come, thy will be done on earth as it is in heaven. Give us this day our daily bread. And forgive us our trespasses, as we forgive those who trespass against us. And lead us not into temptation, but deliver us from evil. For thine is the kingdom, and the power, and the glory, forever." Amen.

Chapter 7

I Am Of Worth

It is very difficult to nurture someone if you have never been nurtured. I have a deep compassion for children, infants, and adults who have been abused. I created a CD, "Enfolded in God's Love," for a project I had to turn in for Miami Valley Hospital, Pastoral Counseling class. I used a hammock for the adult with head phones and enfolded the person in a blanket. The goal was to realize how much we are loved by God and that God will never abandon us. God created our inner most being and we are special in God's sight.

I invite you to picture yourself in a hammock, or lie down on your couch and wrap yourself in a blanket. Jesus was wrapped in swaddling cloths, and you are now wrapped in a blanket enfolded in God's love. You are fearfully and wonderfully made (Psalm 139:14).

Picture being immersed in God's great love. Now feel God's love enfolding you, telling you how much God loves you.

Take a breath and let it soak in. After you take a breath, allow what has kept you in bonds, in knots, to come forth and then just speak it. Let it come out, and name it, _____. Pause.

Give yourself some time. When ready hear these words: As a pastor, I declare "You are forgiven, in the name of Jesus Christ." Believe it, accept it and praise the Lord for God's grace. We don't deserve it but that's grace. Feel God's love enfolding you, immersing you, being *intertwined with Jesus*, you are loved. Allow God's Spirit to nurture and caress you. And remember after all you've been through, God was with you then, and God is with you now. You are *intertwined with Jesus*. Praise God!

"I am of worth," "I am of worth," say it to yourself, "I am of worth," "I am of worth," your name "_____ is of worth!" We fail to grasp how much we are loved by our Lord Jesus. You are part of God's family, you are God's heir as Paul tells us in Romans that you have received a spirit of adoption. "When we cry, 'Abba, Father' (daddy), it is that very Spirit bearing witness with our spirit that we are children of God, and if children, then heirs, heirs of God and joint heirs with Christ" (Romans 8:15b-17).

Nouwen says, "The world tells you many lies about who you are, and you simply have to be realistic enough to remind yourself of this. Every time you feel hurt, offended, or rejected, you have to dare to say to yourself, 'These feelings, strong as they may be, are not telling me the truth about myself. The truth, even though I cannot feel it right now, is that I am the chosen child of God, precious in God's eyes, called the Beloved from all eternity, and held safe in an everlasting embrace.'"

"It was Nouwen's deepest conviction that he (and every person) was chosen by God before the foundations of the earth to be a child of God and called 'my beloved in whom I am well pleased'" (Luke 3:22). His most joyful task and greatest gift was to remind himself and others of their true identify and purpose. "My friends," he would often say, "I tell you that we are loved with a 'first love' even before we are born."

Nouwen says: "One of the tragedies of our life is that we keep forgetting who we are and waste a lot of time and energy to prove what doesn't need to be proved. We are God's beloved daughters and sons, not because we have proven ourselves worthy of God's love, but because God freely chose us." He says that, "when you forget your true identity as a beloved child of God you lose your way in life. Every time you are afraid, you can open yourself to God's presence, hear God's voice again and be brought back to perfect love that cast out fear and brings in greater freedom."

From his book, *The God who Comes,* Carol Carretto says, "You need no longer ask yourself, 'Who am I?' You know it, see it, you live it. By finding God in you, you have found yourself. As you discover the unity and trinity of God within you, you discover and live the unity of your human existence. This brings a sense of peace which is complete and divine. What is left to fear if God is my Father? Now with faith I know what to believe, what to want, what to do. With faith I become 'someone', called by name by God Himself, given my mandate by God Himself."

I am God's beloved. I belong to God's family, I am an heir of the kingdom of God. Let this sink in a little. You are not your own. God has touched you, marked you as God's special child. You are to love Him as a child loves. Claim it. When the devil attacks with false messages, tell the devil to get out, it is not truth, claim your position. I am God's child, I am *intertwined with Jesus.*

Pastor Bobby Schuller, who broadcasts his worship service on the television show called the *Hour of Power,* has written a book, *You are Beloved* about the importance of knowing you are the beloved of God. He declares the following creed has changed his life and the lives of many as you say this daily:

"I'm not what I do. I'm not what I have. I'm not what people say about me. I am the beloved of God. It's who I am. No one can take it from me. I don't have to worry. I don't have to hurry. I can trust my friend Jesus and share his love with the world."

"If you want to be upheld by someone who delights in you, see yourself as one with Jesus by faith. Take on His identity. Be a servant, rest in His love, and rejoice in His will. God already sees you through the lens of His beloved Son; learn to see yourself through the same lens." (Daily Strength).

PRAYER: Oh Lord, I am humbled, for I am of worth because you adopted me as your own. You love me with all my weaknesses, and see me as I sometimes don't see myself, as completely whole. Help me to accept myself as your child, so I can be all that you want me to be through the strength and love of Jesus as I am *intertwined with Jesus.* Amen.

Chapter 8

Our Power: Holy Spirit

The Holy Spirit is the sap or fuel of the vine that helps us, guides us leading us to truth. Jesus tells us, "But the comforter (counselor, helper, intercessor, advocate, strengthener, standby), the Holy Spirit, whom the Father will send in My name {in My place, to represent Me and act on My behalf} He will teach you all things. And He will cause you to recall – will remind you of, bring to your remembrance – everything I have told you (John 14:26 Amplified).

Chambers says about the Holy Spirit, "It is an amazing revelation of the marvelous love and condescension of God, that in Christ Jesus and by the reception of Holy Spirit, He can take us, sin–broken, sin-diseased, wrong creatures, and remake us entirely until we are really the ones in whom the Holy Spirit intercedes as we do our part."

Phillip Keller says, "In our walk with God, we are told explicitly by Christ himself that it would be His Spirit who would be sent to guide us and to lead us into all truth (John 16:13). This same gracious Spirit takes the truth of God, the Word of God, and makes it plain to our hearts and minds and spiritual understanding. It is He who gently, tenderly, but persistently says to us, 'This is the way – walk in it.' And as we comply and cooperate with His gentle promptings, a sense of safety, comfort and well-being envelops us. It is He, too, who comes quietly, but emphatically to make the life of Christ, my Shepherd, real and personal and intimate to me.... The gracious spirit continually brings home to me the acute consciousness that I am God's child and He is my Father."

As we are reading God's Word, a verse will stand out, almost like it is speaking to you. When this happens stop and ponder what the Holy Spirit is saying to you. For "the Word of God is living and active, sharper than any two-edged sword" (Hebrews 4:12).

Underhill tells us, "For a spiritual life is simply a life in which all that we do comes from the center, where we are anchored in God: a life soaked through and through by a sense of His reality and claim, and self- given to the great movement of his will."

The Holy Spirit helps us when we pray. The Word says, "In the same way, the Spirit helps us in our weakness. We do not know what we ought to pray for, but the Spirit himself intercedes for us with groans that words cannot express. And he who searches our hearts knows the mind of the Spirit, because the Spirit intercedes for the saints in accordance with God's will" (Romans 8:26-27 NIV).

Chambers says, "The whole source of our strength is receiving, recognizing and relying on the Holy Spirit." He continues to say, "There are tremendous thoughts expressed in God's Book and unless we have learned to rely on the Holy Spirit we shall say, 'Oh, I shall never understand that.' But the Holy Spirit in us understands it, and as we recognize and rely on Him, He will work it out, whether we consciously understand or not. We have to realize this great revealed thought underneath, that the Holy Spirit is working out in us the mind of God even as He worked out the mind of God in Christ Jesus."

Chambers in his book, *My Utmost for His Highest* says, "The greatest characteristic a Christian can exhibit is this completely unveiled openness before God, which allows that person's life to become a mirror for others. When the Spirit fills us, we are transformed, and by beholding God we become mirrors. You can always tell when someone has been beholding the glory of the Lord, because your inner spirit senses that he mirrors the Lord's own character."

Paul tells us that we can do all things through Christ: I have strength for all things in Christ who empowers me - I am ready for anything and equal to anything through Him who infuses inner strength into me, (that is I am self-sufficient in Christ's sufficiency)"(Philippians 4:13 Amplified Bible).

We can do all things which means we can face all things, what are you facing? Name it here:_____. Jesus is alive and is within us, infusing power within to do all things. Jesus is *intertwined with you and me.* We can do whatever it is that is before us. In some churches at Easter, the hymn is sung, *He Lives.* It asks, *You ask me how I know he lives? He lives within my heart.* Do we not believe it? Yes, we believe it. Now put it into practice. Say: "With the help of Jesus I can face whatever I am facing:_____. I need your help, guidance, and power of the Holy Spirit. I will trust you Jesus to give me the strength as I am *intertwined with you.*"

The Holy Spirit is alive and well within us as we listen and are guided to the Lord's directives. "I will praise the Lord, who counsels me even at night my heart instructs me" (Psalm 16:7 NIV). I have a pencil and paper by my bed so that when an inspiration comes I can write the thought down. If I wait to write it down in the morning it is gone.

I have found when the Holy Spirit calls us and speaks, we receive a "nagging" until we realize it is God calling and directing us to do it. Then we must *do it.* Sometimes I test this request until it becomes so strong I need to listen and obey. It can be as simple as someone coming into my mind, and I stop and pray, call or text, and tell that person I was thinking of them. Or God can tell you how much you should give to him or her in need, or to a charity. Stop, pause, listen as God speaks directs and cautions with a *no* also.

God directs us as we connect with others. Just as God speaks through His Word, and the pastor's sermon, God also speaks as we encounter others at the grocery, at our Bible study small groups, and in other places. It is so awesome when someone says something to you, and you know it is directly from the Lord spoken for you.

Let us pray: O Lord, help me to be bold, to believe in the power of the Holy Spirit as you direct me to do what you have called me to do. As you convict me, help me repent, as you direct me, help me follow. As you bring someone to my mind, help me to pray for them or contact them, if you so direct. Bring to my mind your Word, so it will counsel me and help me in time of need. All this I ask in Jesus' Name. Amen.

Chapter 9

Do It Now!

How do we stay in touch with our Jesus as we are *intertwined with Him*? How? Thomas R. Kelly, a Quaker, in his book, *"A Testament of Devotion"*, tells us to "Begin now, as you read these words, as you are sit in your chair, to offer your whole selves, utterly and in joyful abandon, in quiet, glad surrender to him who is within…. Walk, talk, play, and laugh with your friends. But behind the scenes, keep up the life of simple prayer and inward worship. Keep it up throughout the day. Let inward prayer be your last act before you fall asleep and the first act when you awake." Kelly goes on to say that attending to Jesus' presence is not always easy. He writes, "Lapses are so frequent, the intervals, when we forget Him, so long. Rewarding because we have begun to live."

Kelly says, "Life is meant to be lived from a center, a divine Center." That we all can live a life of amazing power and peace if we really want to. He suggests, "there is a divine abyss within us all, a Holy infinite Center, a Heart, a Life who speaks in us and through us to the world. We have all heard this holy whisper at times. Kelly informs us that it doesn't take time, for it is a life of little whispered words of adoration, of praise, of prayer, of worship that can be breathed all through the day…. One can have a busy day yet remain in the holy presence. There is no new technique, the process grows more simple. We can begin with whispered words like *thine only*. I say *intertwined with Jesus*. Repeat them over and over again and move to praise.

Kelly tells us to begin *now*, "for the *now* contains all that is needed for the absolute satisfaction of our deepest cravings... For within the Now is the dwelling place of God Himself. In the Now we are at home at last... The sense of Presence is as if two beings were joined in one single configuration..." I say, we are *intertwined with Jesus*.

John Eldredge shares, "I find I need to be restored and renewed in Jesus at the end of the day. I wish it weren't so, but I haven't yet learned to abide in Christ all day long, every day... I wander... I strive... I indulge... I forget. It's the whole 'remain in me' thing. I haven't been able to pull it off day after day. So I begin at bedtime by offering myself to Jesus once more, coming back under his authority and covering. The only safe place to be."

We are learning that we are *intertwined with Jesus*. I am finding myself saying *intertwined with Jesus* over and over throughout the day for it helps me connect with my Lord Jesus. It helps me cast out bad thoughts by redirecting my thinking. It awakens me to the awesomeness of being *intertwined*. So say it, say it: "_____ (your name) is *intertwined with Jesus*." Say it many times and see the transformation, renewing of mind, become a reality. Especially when you start to panic, or a sudden rush of insecurity or uncertainty plague you. Stop, pause, take a breath, and say, "I am *intertwined with Jesus*." Then say: "Thank you Jesus." Remember that you are a child of God and Jesus is with you at this moment. You are not alone! Nothing can separate you from Jesus, not death, not illness, nor things impending and threatening, nor things to come (Romans 8:38). Now breathe, tell Jesus what you are experiencing and allow the Holy Spirit to comfort, direct and settle you.

Nouwen says not to be surprised with all the distractions, "It will take a while for these countless distractions to disappear, but eventually they will, especially when they realize that you refuse to open the door to them. We do not fight distractions by pushing things away, we fight them by focusing on one thing, like the scripture you are reading. When distractions come, smile at them, let them pass and return to the text."

Kelly summarizes by saying, "Life from the center is a life of unhurried peace and power. It is simple. It is serene. It is amazing. It is triumphant. It is radiant. It takes no time, but it occupies all our time. And it makes our life programs new and overcoming. We need not get frantic. He is at the helm. And when our little day is done we lie down quietly in peace, for all is well."

Be kind to yourself as you become aware and catch yourself. Lose no time in self-recrimination but breathe and give a silent prayer for forgiveness and start again, just where you are. Pray, "Oh Jesus, come, I want you ever present, help me be more aware of your presence this day. I am *intertwined* with you."

Let us Pray: O Lord, I am *intertwined with Jesus*, I can hardly take it in. I am *intertwined*, wrapped, securely with and in You. I don't have to worry, or be in a hurry, I can call on you Jesus and you are right here. Help me to remember throughout the day, you are within, and all I have to do is call to you Jesus. Thank you Jesus, Amen.

Chapter 10

Discipline

The Lord disciplines those that God loves (Hebrews 12:5-6). We have heard this and we all quiver, for who likes to be disciplined? First of all, we want it "my way" and being disciplined refutes it.

God disciplines us for our good that we may share in his holiness (Hebrew 12:10-13). Learning to hear God's voice and walking with God take time and practice. For example, John Eldredge in his book, *Walking with God*, says, "If you want to make music, you have to learn how to play an instrument. And in the beginning, it doesn't sound too good…. But if you hang in there, you come to enjoy it… This includes our walk with God. It takes time and practice. It's awkward at first… But if we hang in there, we do begin to get it, and as it becomes more and more natural, our lives are filled with His presence and all the joy and beauty and pleasure that comes with it. It is something to be learned. And it is worth learning." He continues to say, "An intimate conversational walk with God is available and… requires communication."

It takes discipline to meet with our Lord every day. It takes discipline to remember to whom you belong. You are the beloved. Declare it by calling it out when the evil one tells you differently. It takes discipline to remember you are *intertwined with Jesus* and know Jesus is present with you every moment.

Nouwen tells us "discipleship calls for discipline, and you can't have one without the other. They share the same linguistic root from which means, 'to learn from.'

Prayer is the discipline of the moment. For when we pray we enter into the presence of God whose name is God-with-us. Listening to the voice of God requires us to direct our minds and hearts toward that voice with all our attention." How? Nouwen says to do what we are talking about – "take a simple prayer, a sentence or a word and slowly repeat it. We can use the Lord's Prayer, or name of Jesus," I say *intertwined with Jesus*. Nouwen encourages us by saying: "When we remain faithful to our discipline, even if it is only ten minutes a day we gradually come to see that there is a space within where God dwells and where we are invited to dwell with God. Once we come to know that inner, holy place we want to be there and be spiritually fed."

Nouwen says, "To live the spiritual life and to let God's presence fill us takes constant prayer. To move from our illusions and isolations back to that place in our heart where God continues to form us in the likeness of Christ takes time and attention. Once your body, mind and heart are reunited in prayer your whole life will become an act of thanksgiving and praise."

Oswald Chambers in his book, *My Utmost for His Highest* tells us that "Discipleship means personal, passionate devotion to a person – our Lord Jesus Christ. To be a disciple is to be a devoted bondservant motivated by the love for the Lord Jesus." He says, "No one on earth has this passionate love for our Lord Jesus unless the Holy Spirit has given it to him. We may admire, respect, and revere him, but we cannot love him on our own. The only One who truly loves the Lord Jesus is the Holy Spirit and it is He who has 'poured out in our hearts the very love of God" (Romans 5:15).

Foster says, "The primary requirement for spiritual disciplines is a longing after God." As noted In Psalm 42:1-2 (NIV), "As the deer pants for streams of water, so my soul pants for you, O God. My soul thirsts for God, for the living God." Foster continues to say, "The purpose of the Disciplines is liberation from the stifling slavery to self-interest and fear. When one's inner spirit is set free from all that holds it down, that can hardly be described as dull drudgery. Singing, dancing, even shouting characterize the Disciplines of the spiritual life... When we genuinely believe that inner transformation is God's work and not ours we can put to rest our passion to set others straight."

William Barclay says: "Abiding in Christ means staying in close contact with Jesus which makes them fruitful branches. For the greatest glory of the Christian life is that by our life and conduct we can bring glory to God."

From *Illustrations Unlimited*: James Montgomery
"Prayer is the soul's sincere desire,
Uttered or unexpressed –
The motion of a hidden fire,
That trembles in the breast.
Prayer is the burden of a sigh,
The falling of a tear,
The upward glancing of an eye,
When none but God is near.

Chapter 11

Inter(Twin)ed With Jesus

When the Lord called me to write the book, *Intertwined - Beverly and Barbara in the Womb*, I said, "Oh my Lord, I have never written a book before. Barbara only lived five minutes and it was 75 years ago. Really, me? Now?" The call was so strong and I completed the book.

In the book, I state that as a fetus I became aware, I became conscious that another or something else was beside me. As I became more aware, we poked each other, we laughed, had our own language, and we were *intertwined.* I was the aggressive one, Barbara was the quiet one and preferred her own little corner.

Oh, my Jesus, you are right here beside me now. So real, so present, I am the one that needs to be awakened. You are here within me every moment. I just can't picture you that ordinary. You know all, "You know when I sit down and when I rise up; you discern my thoughts; ... Even before a word is on my tongue You, Lord, know it completely. You hem me in, behind and before, and lay your hand upon me. For it was you who formed my inward parts; you knit me together in my mother's womb. I praise you for I am fearfully and wonderfully made. My frame was not hidden from you when I was being made in secret, intricately woven in the depths of the earth. Your eyes beheld my unformed substance" (Psalm 139:2, 5, 13-16).

Young says it so well in her book, *Jesus Calling*, "I am Christ in You, *the hope* of *Glory*. The One who walks beside you, holding you by your hand, is the same One who lives within you. This is a deep unfathomable mystery. You and I are *intertwined* in an intimacy involving every fiber of your being. The Light of My Presence shines within you, as well as upon you."

Prayer: O Lord, You are right here in the midst of it all, wanting my attention. I was starved for attention after Barbara died, and you must be wanting my attention also. Oh Jesus help me include you in the every day, every moment occurrences. Help me remember you are living within.

I am *intertwined with Jesus,* and you are *intertwined with Jesus.* Now continue your prayer as the Holy Spirit directs you saying what is on your heart. Then close with the Lord's Prayer: "Our Father who art in heaven, hallowed be thy name. Thy kingdom come, thy will be done on earth as it is in heaven. Give us this day our daily bread. And forgive us our trespasses, as we forgive those who trespass against us. And lead us not into temptation, but deliver us from evil. For thine is the kingdom, and the power, and the glory, forever." Amen.

Chapter 12

The Mind

Stop and think about what you are thinking about. Joyce Meyer says, "For most of my life, I didn't think about what I was thinking about. I simply thought whatever fell into my head. I had no revelation that Satan could inject thoughts into my mind. Much of what was in my head was either lies that Satan was telling me or just plain nonsense-things that really were not worth spending my time thinking about. The devil was controlling my life because he was controlling my thoughts."

Meyer continues to say, "One thing the Lord told me when He began to teach me about the battlefield of the mind, became a major turning point for me. The Lord said, 'Think about what you're thinking about.' As I began to do so, it was not long before I began to see why I was having so much trouble in my life. My mind was a mess!"

Stop and think about what you are thinking about. Press your alert button – Caution. Do you keep thinking over and over in your mind your last event? Or on something that happened to you last month or last year and you just can't stop thinking about it? Or do some strange, crazy things just come out of nowhere into your thinking? As you start paying attention to your thoughts, stop the thought before it turns into a mountain of anger, resentment, jealousy, or bitterness.

"Thinking about what you're thinking about is very valuable because Satan usually deceives people into thinking that the source of their misery or trouble is something other than what it really is." Meyer continues to say, "He wants them to think they are unhappy due to what is going on around them (their circumstances), but the misery is actually due to what is going on inside them (their thoughts)."

I have found it to be so helpful to be more aware of my thoughts and take every thought captive (2 Corinthians 10:5). When these thoughts come, seek Jesus' opinion, ask Jesus about this thought. If the thought is destructive, then command the thought to leave in Jesus' Name. Say: "Get out of here Satan, I am the beloved of Christ, I did not bring this thought to my mind and I denounce it in the Name of Jesus." Then breathe. Let it go. You may have to do this several (or even many) times for Satan likes to attack us where we are most vulnerable.

Paul tells us: "Do not conform any longer to the pattern of this world but be transformed by the renewing of your mind. Then you will be able to test and approve what God's will is-his good, pleasing and perfect will" (Romans 12:2 NIV).

When a thought or something whispers, "You are not smart enough to do that, you just goofed, or you know she doesn't want to be your friend" you make assumptions and agreements that they are true.

Eldredge says, "By 'agreements' I mean those subtle convictions we come to assent to, give way to, or are raised to assume are true. It happens down deep in our souls where our real beliefs about life are formed... And something in us responds, *That's true.* We make an agreement with it, and a conviction is formed."

This is serious because these false assumptions can become what we believe to be true and our life commandment. I chose my college major under a false agreement that had become instilled in me. We need to become alert to these false thoughts, cast them out and not believe them. Yes, we can be our worse bully.

Do you have some false assumptions that have become your life commandment? Pause and reflect – what are they? Maybe someone said that you are stupid, not capable of a task, or there was a friendship difficulty and you felt rejected and not worthy of friendship. So you relented in agreement and acknowledged that you were not good in relationships? These assumptions are untrue.

Now when ready name your false assumptions _____.

Let us pray: Oh Lord, I have been living with assumptions that are not true about myself, false statements that I have come to believe to be true. Help me get rid of these messages that haunt me, hurt me, tear me down, make me feel like I can't measure up. Cast them out In Jesus' Name as I become aware of these statements. In Jesus' Name I denounce _____ (untruth). Free me from this thought for I am *intertwined with you*, Jesus, and it is not true. Free me and replace it with your correctness; that I am your child and can do all things through Christ and the power of Holy Spirit. Thank you for helping me see truth and to live in it. That I can Call on You, and You will erase it so the thought is gone and I am no longer under its control. In Jesus' Name I pray, Amen.

"Summing it all up friends, I'd say you'll do best by filling your minds and meditating on things true, noble, reputable, authentic, compelling, gracious-the best, not the worst, the beautiful, not the ugly; things to praise, not things to curse. Put into practice what you learned from me, what you heard and saw and realized. Do that, and

God who makes everything work together, will work you into his most excellent harmonies (Philippians 4:8-9, The Message).

Meyers says, "Positive minds produce positive lives. Negative minds produce negative lives. Positive thoughts are always full of faith and hope. Negative thoughts are always full of fear and doubt." She continues to state that, "It is by this continual 'watching over' your thoughts that you begin to take every thought captive unto the obedience of Jesus Christ (2 Corinthians10:5 KJV). The Holy Spirit is quick to remind you if your mind is beginning to take you in a wrong direction, then the decision becomes yours. Will you flow in the mind of the flesh or in the mind of the Spirit? One leads to death, the other to life. The choice is yours. Choose life."

"A Happy heart is good medicine and a cheerful mind works healing… You have a powerful source of happiness within you: the Holy Spirit! He can empower you to live above your circumstances. When your heart is heavy, ask Him to fill it with buoyant cheerfulness. He takes pleasure in doing this as you entrust yourself into His capable care. Your heart and mind are intricately connected. It is impossible to have a happy heart when your mind is full of negative thoughts. Left to itself, your mind can become "the devil's workshop" – pulling you away from Me. This is why you need to exert control over your thinking. Ask the Holy Spirit to help you; invite Him to control your mind…. As I refresh your mind with promises of My constant Love and the eternal home awaiting you, heavenly Light shines powerfully into your heart. Bask in this cheery Light, while My healing Presence permeates you deeply – all the way down to your bones!" (From Jesus Lives)

Foster tells us, "The decision to set the mind on the higher things of life is an act of the will. It is the result of a consciously chosen way of thinking and living."

Praise the Lord, the Lord is with us helping us set our minds on what is true. Be diligent in asking for the Lord's help to cast out what is false and live as God's beloved child *intertwined with Jesus*!

Chapter 13

The Pit

Oh, Lord, I'm screaming, I'm _____ I just don't have words. I am zoned out. I just got word I didn't pass my final test. My doctor just told me that _____. I just had a misunderstanding with _____. I don't know why, I just feel sad, depressed: _____. You fill in the blanks.

Oh Lord, this is too much. Why Lord? How can I continue Lord? Where are you? And there is silence – silence ----or a knock on the door. Oh God, S-O-S. Pause and you fill in the blanks_____.

Where do I turn when life gets overwhelming? I fall on my knees, go to the chapel, turn to scripture (NRSV):

Psalm 28:1-2: "To you, O Lord, I call; my rock, do not refuse to hear me, for if you are silent to me, I shall be like those who go down to the Pit. Hear the voice of my supplication as I cry for help."

Psalm 27:7-8: "Hear, O Lord, when I cry aloud, be gracious to me and answer me! "Come," my heart says, "seek his face!" Your face, Lord do I seek. Do not hide your face from me."

Psalm 91:1-4: "You who live in the shelter of the Most High, who abide in the shadow of the Almighty, will say to the Lord, "My refuge and my fortress; my God in whom I trust." For he will deliver you from the snare of the fowler and from deadly pestilence; he will cover you with his pinions (feathers), and under his wings you will find refuge; his faithfulness is a shield and buckler."

Isaiah 41:10: "Do not fear, for I am with you, do not be afraid for I am your God; I will strengthen you, I will help you, I will uphold you with my victorious right hand."

Psalm 42:11: "Why are you cast down, O my soul, why are you so disquieted within me? Hope in God; for I shall again praise him, my help and my God."

1 Peter 5:7-9: "Cast all your anxiety on him, because he cares for you. Discipline yourselves, keep alert. Like a roaring lion your adversary, the devil prowls around, looking for someone to devour. Resist him, steadfast in your faith, for you know that your brothers and sisters in all the world are undergoing the same kinds of suffering."

Phillip Keller in his book, *A Shepherd looks at Psalm 23* tells us that "there is an exact parallel to this in caring for sheep. Only those intimately acquainted with sheep and their habits understand the significance of a 'cast' sheep or a 'cast down' sheep. This is an old English shepherd's term for a sheep that has turned over on its back and cannot get up again by itself.... If the owner does not arrive on the scene within a reasonable short time, the sheep will die." So the shepherd faithfully seek his sheep that are lost to find them in case they are downcast and die.

Keller continues to say, "Jesus as our shepherd has the same identical sensations of anxiety, concern and compassion for cast down men and women as I had for cast down sheep." Jesus looked with compassion with down and out individuals for whom society had no use, and he wept. As the good shepherd picking up cast down sheep with tenderness, love and patience He used to restore Peter's soul after his denial. "And so Jesus comes quietly, gently, reassuringly to me no matter when or where or how I may be cast down."

Keller states, "As for sheep there is nothing that quiets a sheep and gives peace and assurance as the presence of the shepherd. As in our life as Christian, there is no substitute for this keen awareness that my shepherd is nearby. There is nothing like Christ's presence to dispel the fear, panic, and terror of the unknown."

Psalm 28:6-7: "Blessed be the Lord, for he has heard the sound of my pleadings. The Lord is my strength and my shield; in him my heart trusts."

(I Corinthians 10:13 NIV): "No temptation has seized you except what is common to man. And God is faithful; he will not let you be tempted beyond what you can bear. But when you are tempted he will also provide a way out so that you can stand up under it." Hold on to these promises, for God is faithful and is with you through all things. So claim them as God's beloved.

"Fearfulness is a form of bondage. I died on the cross for you so that you would not be a slave to fear… It isn't easy to break free from fearfulness. However, the Spirit of adoption can help you in this struggle, enabling you to see yourself as you truly are: a much-loved child of God! The Spirit frees you to cry out, "Abba, Father," believing you are God's precious, adopted child…. Let Him hold you close to His Abba-heart, where you know you are safe. Open your heart to receive vast quantities of God's love. The more of this Love you hold in your heart, the less room there is for fear" (Romans 8:15-17) (*Jesus Lives*).

To find release when you are downcast:

Breathe – Say: "God is with me." Where else can you run, but into the loving arms of your God and Savior?

God is with you even in your doubts:

Pause

Breathe – I love you!

Now allow God to enfold you and hear God whisper: "I am here, I am here, you are not alone, I love you."

Sometimes we also need other people to help us through the rough times. Remember friends carried their paralyzed friend to Jesus to be healed. At times we have to be carried and allow others to pray for us and receive their care. For the prayers of our friends are powerful as you feel them carry you in their prayers.

What else can I do?

Talk with your pastor, get a Stephen minister from your church or inquire about their services, they are so helpful.

Call your physician.

Call or see your counselor. If you do not have a counselor, get one.

Share with a trusted, confidential friend.

Join a confidential support group or Bible study group.

It is so helpful to spend time with your church family in worship. God gave us the church, God's people to strengthen and encourage one another and build each other up (2 Thessalonians 5:11).

You can make a reminder to yourself from Scripture for encouragement. See Psalm 16, type it and put it on your mirror or someplace you see it often. You could use any of the above scripture in this way. Choose one that speaks to your heart, and place it where you can see it.

I can just hear you tell me, "Stop it, enough already!" It is a process. Moving out of the pit is a process. We take our journey one day at a time and do not rush it. We are lifted up as we fall into the arms of our Lord, as we allow others in, as we begin to breathe again, and as we remember we are *intertwined with Jesus* never to be separated from Him. For neither death, nor illness, nor calamity can separate us from the love of Jesus (Romans 8:35, 38-39).

Prayer: Come Lord Jesus, come. Fill my soul with your presence. I don't understand why my soul is so downcast. I need You to lift up my soul, to caress, to strengthen and to bring calmness. Help me to realize I am not alone, You are right here, *intertwined* with me bringing a semblance of togetherness. I am so thankful for Your presence this day. Help me arise with an air of thankfulness for all that You have done for me this day and every day. Now: Add your own need, concerns and request here_____ _____. In Jesus' Name I pray, Amen.

Chapter 14

Suicide

"Oh Lord, I am overwhelmed, there seems to be no end to this. I am beside myself. Every day is insane. How, Oh, how do I go on?"

It is like my own Red Sea is before me and other things, terrible things approaching me from behind. I am cornered, boxed in all around, all I want to do is scream. I am walking in my darkest, deepest valley and there is fear all around. You said you would be with me, where are you?"

I am crying uncontrollably! Crying in so much pain I don't care about living! The pain is so intense I don't care what others may think. I am just hurting so badly. S-O-S. Take a breath. Stop! Get help - call 1-800-273-8233 or **suicidepreventionlifeline.org** NOW!

Lay your weapon down, whatever weapon it may be: drugs, a gun, knife, a rope. Do it now. Ask someone to help you lay them down, and take them out of the house. Life looks helpless this minute, but another minute in a different day will be different. You say, "No, I don't care. You don't understand." Scream, let it go. Take a breath. Breathe. Move, get yourself out: move, change your thought, breathe.

Pray – "Help me, O Lord! Help me Jesus."

Take a walk.

Pray: "I am yours." Breathe. Walk.

Say: "I am your beloved. Even if I think no one loves me, You do Lord. I am Loved, I am *intertwined with Jesus.*" Accept this. Pray.

If you have you have not sought help, DO IT NOW! Call: *1-800-273-8233* or **suicidepreventionlifeline.org.**

Yes, it takes courage, but do it NOW, not tomorrow - NOW.

Robert J. Morgan says, "The Red Sea may roll before us; the desert may entrap us; the enemy may press on our heels. The past may seem implausible and the future impossible, but God works in ways we cannot see. He will make a way of escape for His weary, but waiting, children." "I the Lord will even make a way in the wilderness, and rivers in the desert" (Isaiah 43:19 KJV).

David was in the pit. God heard his cry. God drew him up from the desolate pit, out of the miry bog (Psalm 40: 1b-2).

Pause – Be still – Stop.

"Do not fear, for I am with you, do not be afraid, for I am your God. I will strengthen you, I will help you. I will uphold you with my victorious right hand" (Isaiah 41:10).

"Do not fear, for I have redeemed you; I have called you by name; you are mine. When you pass through the waters, I will be with you; and through the rivers, they shall not overwhelm you! When you walk through fire, you shall not be burned, and the flame shall not consume you. For I am the Lord your God, the holy one of Israel, your Savior... Because you are precious in my sight, and honored, and I love you." (Isaiah 43:1-4).

Jesus comes and takes you by the hand. Allow Jesus to come and take you by the hand. Reach out your hand and allow Jesus to take it. Breathe. Jesus is your HOPE, your anchor. Hold on, Keep holding on, saying: Jesus is my Hope. Jesus is my Hope. I am *intertwined with You, Jesus.* Now ask Jesus to help you reach out for Help.

Now call: 1-800-273-8233. You are loved. You are *intertwined with Jesus.* You are loved.

This is my prayer for you. O Lord, come. Lord Jesus, help this person who is reading this now. You have promised to be with us, to never abandon us. Come and touch, come and show yourself to this person. Show your child that you love him or her. Help this child know he or she is loved. You will never do harm, but will caress, enfold, embrace your beloved child in your love. Thank you Lord for saving them now. In Jesus' Name. Amen.

Please call for help for your loved one's sake, your wife, husband, mom, dad, girl/boyfriend, grandma, grandpa, friend, neighbor. Call for them or call one of them! Even though you don't know it, they love you! Please give them another chance.

Chapter 15

Loving Oneself

"Love," we just can't comprehend the depth of love Jesus, our Lord, and Holy Spirit has for us. Jesus' love and presence are inseparable. Because Jesus lives in us there is no limit to the depth of intimacy we can experience with Jesus. Jesus is alive within and knows everything about us – when we sit, sleep, talk, walk, including our deepest desires and darkest secrets.

Are you shaking, trembling with all kind of emotion? Jesus knows and sees all, and still loves us in spite of our imperfections, weaknesses and shortcomings. It is a definition of love not defined or found in Webster's Dictionary. We know that Jesus died for us, clearing all past and present things in our lives making us right (righteous) before God. We don't deserve this gift but that is what we call grace. We are okay. It is as simple as that. We are more than okay. We are perfect in God's sight through Jesus our Lord.

Now, right now begin to accept "you." If you have not loved yourself, begin now to love yourself. Throw your fears away. Accept yourself and begin anew. Be that loving person God created you to be.

Jesus said, "You are to love others as yourself," (Matt 22:39). How can you love others, if you do not love you? Be kind to yourself. Feel embraced with Jesus' arms around you and hear Jesus whispering to you, "I love you, you are mine – forever." You are loved, so love yourself as God created you - you! Then you can love others. So smile, open doors, welcome others, and do unto others as you would want them to do to you. I ask you, "How do you want to be treated? Do you want to be treated with respect, kindness, and thoughtfulness?" Maybe it's time for a sit down talk with your husband, wife, children, siblings, friends, boy/girlfriend, mother, father, or significant person in your life?

Now: Be still, breathe, and say, I am *intertwined with Jesus*. Rest, and listen to our Lord. "You are connected to Me by Love-bonds that nothing can sever. However, you may sometimes feel alone, because your union with Me is invisible. Ask Me to open your eyes, so that you can find Me everywhere. The more aware you are of My Presence, the safer you feel" (*Jesus Calling*).

Let us pray: O Lord, help me to love myself. Thank you for loving me and making it possible for me through the Holy Spirit to love you and to love others. I praise your Holy Name. Help me to accept your grace, your forgiveness, your mercy and your great love. Help me remember I belong to you. (Add whatever is on your heart: _____.) In Jesus' Name, Amen.

Chapter 16

Divorce or Loss of Spouse

Living as a divorced woman is not easy. Divorce was not God's plan but divorce happens. I felt guilt breaking my wedding vows that were given in the presence of my Lord, family and friends. Other times, I felt relief and thankful for family support. I also felt like I was walking around as a half person because we had become *one*. So I decided to plan to become one and whole again. I invited Jesus to restore my oneness. I literally got on the floor and invited Jesus to enter my other half to become *intertwined with Jesus*. This became a fusion that you can picture as Jesus came and made me one person again.

If you find yourself alone now, after losing your spouse or loved one through death or divorce. I invite you to lie on the floor or couch, and get comfortable, pause, take a breath, and speak to Jesus whatever is on your heart. Let your honesty speak and pray. If you want to ask for forgiveness do, then accept God's grace, for you are forgiven. When ready, ask Jesus to come, and fill your void. Ask Jesus to enter your other side and make you whole, *one*. Picture Jesus coming to this side, to complete it. Now thank Jesus for doing so, realizing that you are one person again. Rejoice, and continue to thank Jesus, your Lord, and the Spirit for making this possible. Rest and get up a new person when ready.

Young expresses Jesus' words to us in *Jesus Lives*: "My commitment to you, which is deeper and stronger than even the most ardent wedding vows. No matter how passionately in love a bride and groom may be, their vows last only until one of them dies. My commitment, however, is absolutely unlimited. When you asked me to be your Savior, I wed you for eternity."

From *Daily Strength* WEEC Devotional, on September 18, 2017, we can read: "The Beloved Servant": "We are in Him and He is in us. We take on His name as a bride takes the name of her husband. We are filled with God's Spirit in the same way Jesus was filled with His Spirit. As with the mystery of marriage, two become one. We and Jesus are inseparable."

Pray this prayer, or one of your own: Oh Lord Jesus come and restore wholeness to me. I feel so alone, so broken, so empty. I need you to unite my being and bring peace. Come now, Lord Jesus and *intertwine* your presence with mine and make me whole. In Jesus' Name. Amen.

Chapter 17

Grief

My daughter, Christine died, May 12, 2014, from cancer. She suffered so, but stayed in intimate contact with her Lord Jesus, and the Holy Spirit. At her death and afterward, I groaned, moaned, made strange noises, and wept. I did not know what one went through when they grieved. I remember at Mary/Martha's time of grieving, many of her friends were present to grieve with them (John 11:31).

Bishop T. D. Jakes mentioned on his television program during his time of grieving, that what helped him the most was when a person just came and sat and wept with him, not saying a mumbling word.

I cried to our Lord, "Why, why, she was only 43 years old, she wanted to serve you. Where are you God?" God came, for God is the God who comes and enfolds you. God says, "I am here I will not abandon you, you are mine, come and rest and let me take your heavy burden" (Matthew 11:28).

Jesus comes and whispers: "I know the pain and sorrow you are feeling, and I want you to *pour out your heart* in My Presence. You need to release all those emotions in a safe place... Remember that I am a *Man of sorrows, fully acquainted with grief.* Because of all I suffered, I can empathize with you and share your pain. As you pour out your emotions in my Presence, your heavy burden grows lighter. You no longer carry your sorrows alone. You release them to Me, and I then *relieve and refresh your soul....* Linger a while in My Presence, letting my Love soak into your soul." (*Jesus Lives*)

I believed in God's healing and had led many healing services. Even at the very end when Christine was all skin and bones, I believed that God could heal her, but it was not to be. Like grapes on the vine, I was crushed. I cried out, "Oh Jesus, where are you?" And Jesus said, "I am right here weeping with you."

It is important to cry, to let it out, to not keep it all in, to release it. As I released it and cried, I found it gets better, for the Lord was always with me. Now I can advise others: Be *intertwined with Jesus.* Say it often, and find relief. God loves you.

Nouwen discuses grief saying: "This is what mourning is all about: allowing the pain of our losses to enter our hearts; having courage to let our wounds be known to ourselves and felt by ourselves; embracing the freedom to cry in anguish, or to scream in protest, - and so to risk being led into an inner space where the joy can be found."

Billy Graham states that, "grief is a reality. Our loved one who died may be better off, when in heaven, but we aren't better off." He says, "A major part of our lives has been ripped from us, and just as it takes time to heal from a major surgery, so it takes time to heal from the loss of loved ones." He gives four steps to deal with grief: (1) Not to be surprised by our grief, not to deny it, or feel guilty, for it is a process and takes time to heal. (2) To look to the future and accept what has happened. Then little by little learn to live with it. (3) To begin to reach out and help others when ready. And (4) take our burden of grief to our Lord.

Grief relief can be found in the list of these scriptures in my book, *Intertwined, Beverly and Barbara in the Womb.* Start reading and meditating on these passages: Psalm 18:16,19,

Psalm 25:1, Psalm 22:19, Psalm 27:1, Psalm 28:6-9, Psalm 40:1-3 Psalm 30, Psalm 91, Psalm 147, and John 14:27. Pick up your hymnal and read or sing a hymn after reading one or more of the above scriptures. Go to the Lord in prayer and tell it like it is for you.

May God bless you, may God enfold you in God's arms and bring you comfort and peace.

Let us pray: O Lord, may your Holy Spirit speak for me with groanings that words can't express. Intercede as you search my heart and know the pain that I bear. Comfort me, O Lord. Enfold me in your deep embrace. Help me to just sit awhile in your presence and be still. In Jesus' Name. Amen.

Chapter 18

God Winks

I love to see the God winks, the God moments, and the God glances in my life. As our Lord becomes so real, we observe how God is blessing us. God is reciprocal to us by blessing us with those indescribable moments, some call coincidences.

In his book, *When God Winks at You*, Squire Rushnell describes God winks as: "Every time you receive what some call a coincidence or an answered prayer, it is a direct and personal message of reassurance from God to you. It is a sign that you're never alone. In fact, you're always on his GPS – global positioning system I like to call God's Positioning System."

My neighbor shared her God wink with me: "My daughter called to alert me that my nineteen-year-old grandson had gotten a tattoo. "Oh, goodness. What and where?" was my response. My daughter said that he wanted to show me himself. When I stopped by their home the next day, he came bounding out of the house and excitedly exclaimed, "Memaw I got a tattoo!" He promptly displayed his bicep with a tattoo written in script — Proverbs 3:5. When I asked the significance of it, he said, "Don't you recognize it? It's your handwriting?" He then pulled from his wallet a slip of paper I had written that passage for him when he was experiencing some perplexing and confusing times in high school. He told me that it always meant a lot to him. He showed it to the artist, who scanned it, enlarged it and copied it onto his arm. "Memaw, you and that scripture will always be a part of me." Through my tears and to give the moment a bit of frivolity, I gave him a hug and told him I was glad I spelled it right! You never know what impact your actions or words may have on your loved ones. He had never mentioned me slipping him that piece of paper but after all these years it was still meaningful and will remain with him forever."

One of my God winks was very awesome and lifesaving. The day started out fine. I had lunch with Pastor Katya. We met with Julie, liaison with Delaware Sheriff Department to discuss the drug epidemic. In the afternoon, I had my devotions on the patio. At 6:40 p.m. I went to our clubhouse to play bridge. Then all of a sudden I just didn't feel right. I told my neighbor, Bill, and he called the squad. I was taken to the closest emergency department. After tests, it was determined that I had a tear in the aorta (heart) and needed emergency surgery. The doctor informed me that a team would be waiting and ready for me at the hospital. As I entered surgery, the doctor told me later that my aorta started to rupture. He informed me that I was at the right place, at the right time and if I had not been there, I would have died. I praise God for this God moment.

When I met people after surgery, they said to me that God must have had a reason for you to live. I smiled, for God had told me four days prior to the surgery, as I read the Upper Room article, that I was to write this book *Intertwined with Jesus*. This God wink gave me added assurance that I had a purpose and would live. Look for your God winks.

G. May in his book, *The Awakened Heart*, says to ask God directly to shower you with his glances, to remind you of God.

Let us Pray: O Lord Jesus, You are awesome, You come and show Yourself in unbelievable ways. Help us to see You in these God moments and give You the praise. Thank You for revealing yourself to us. Give us eyes to see You and then give You the praise and glory. In Jesus' Name we pray. Amen.

Chapter 19

Rubber Bands

"And in Him all things hold together" (Colossians 1:10).

"I drew them with gentle cords, with bands of love, and I was to them as those who take the yoke from their neck. I stooped and fed them" (Hosea 11:4).

Rubber bands, just plain ordinary rubber bands, have served for me like finding a lucky penny. When I see a rubber band I first acknowledge it, then thank God. You see, it signifies to me that Jesus is holding all things together. I don't know when seeing rubber bands became an awareness of Jesus holding all things together. But when it became a reality I was finding rubber bands in the most unusual places. I must have been going through a trying time for I was finding them often. Oh, it made me smile and breathe a sigh of relief. Each rubber band served as a reminder that Jesus is right here with me through it all, and said to me, "Just don't forget – Jesus is here." Now, you are reading this, so you will begin to find and see rubber bands on the street, under your chair, by the crib, by the tire, in the garage, anywhere. Surprise! So acknowledge, praise, be thankful, and remember Jesus is with you, *intertwined!*

Pray: Oh Jesus, how thankful we are that You are holding all things together. The world seems so in turmoil, our little worlds so exhausting. It brings us comfort and peace to know that You are in control. For You are our refuge and strength, a very present help in trouble. Therefore we will not fear, though the earth should change, though the mountains shake in the heart of the sea. For You are in the midst of it all and will help when the morning dawns. As nations are in uproar, the Lord of hosts is with us. Help us to *be still* and *know* that You are God. That the Lord of hosts is with us; the God of Jacob is our refuge. In Jesus' Name, we pray (Psalm 46). Amen.

Chapter 20

Pots and Pans and Diapers Too

"Lord of all pots and pans and things… Make me a saint by getting meals and washing up the plates!" *A Pilgrim's Prayer* – Brother Lawrence

Brother Lawrence practiced the presence of God continually at his job in the kitchen doing dishes. In his book, *The Practice of the Presence of God*, he felt that "the most excellent method he had found of going to God was that of dong common business without any view of pleasing men and (as far as we are capable) purely for the love of God."

Oh, how I remember changing my daughter's diaper and questioning my "job" and asking, "When Lord can I do what you have called me to do?" But I was already doing it. As I look back, it was my most important job, being "mom." As mom we are helping shape our child as God wants, and God is shaping us. God is working in us and in our child to become whom God desires. It can also be a time to "practice the presence of God" as we fold clothes, do dishes, and nurse or bottle feed our child. That is our "job" now.

Brother Lawrence said: "I find myself often attached with greater sweetness and delight than that of an infant at the mother's breast; so that, if I dare use the expression, I should choose to call this state the bosom of God, for the inexpressible sweetness which I taste and experience there."

What an honor to have this closeness with your child, your mom, or your dad. Take a breath. Relax. Allow yourself to enjoy these precious moment(s) with your infant and with God!

Pray: O God, how precious these moments are with our children. Help us see from your eyes these special times as *called* to serve you in a humbling way. Give us wisdom, give us direction as we see all our sacred moments directed by you as we seek you and listen. Help us not to get discouraged as we underestimate their value. Help us pause, take a breath and experience your very presence as we are *intertwined with you, Jesus.* In Jesus' Name we pray, Amen.

Chapter 21

Rest

"Come away to a deserted place all by yourself and rest awhile" (Mark 6: 31). Come find a quiet place and be still and know I am God (Psalm 46:10). God programmed this time, this day, this sabbath to stop, pause, and let the burdens slide off and rest in God.

"Come to Me just as you are. Let Me enfold you in My compassionate embrace. I know the depth and breadth of your weariness. I see you from the inside out, as well as from the outside in. Nothing about you escapes My attention – or My tender concern. I offer you rest. My child, but in order to receive it you must stop for a time and simply wait with me.... Discipline yourself to stop whatever you are doing and take time to *fix your thoughts on Me*. I provide rest not only for your mind and body but also *for your soul*. However your body and soul cannot rest until your mind settles down. Take quiet, slow breaths while you focus your attention on Me. It can be helpful to say a simple prayer such as: "Jesus fill me with your Peace."…. This transfers your burdens to My strong shoulders" (*Jesus Lives*). I would add as I pray: "I am intertwined with Jesus".

In his book, *Walking with God*, John Eldredge is forced to slow down and pause, for it is raining and this has messed up his vacation plans. Yet he discovers that this is God's plan for him to slow down and stop pushing. As he is sitting on the porch with God, he notices that "there is a life out of which everything flows, a life that comes from God"…. He reflects to the vine and branches (John 15:5) that "life which flows from the vine through branches, is where we get the fruit. The branches are merely channels and life does not exist in the branches themselves, we get it from God." He relates this with his discovery that *rest* is one of the ways we receive this life from God. He encourages us to stop weekly, put our schedules down and be replenished. Eldredge says, "I know that if I will live more intimately with Jesus and follow his voice, I will have a much better chance of finding the life I long for."

"Come to me all you who are weary and burdened, and I will give you REST. Take my yoke upon you and learn from me, for I am gentle and humble in heart, and you will find REST for your souls. For my yoke is easy and my burden is light" (Matthew 11: 28). The yoke is connecting you along the side of Jesus, the two working together, yoked, like being *intertwined with Jesus*. As we give all our burdens to Jesus and we are connected to him we can find rest.

"The Sabbath is "about having a day where you focus on being rather than being productive," (Lynne Baab, *Daily Strength*).

So do something relaxing with the children, enjoy the day, take a break from the routine. Enjoy each moment, for you have this moment today. Give our Lord the praise. And bring your praises to our Lord in your place of worship.

Prayer: O Lord, we thank You for rest. Help us to stop, reflect, look around, and remember you our Creator. Help us to stop and listen to the birds that sing to us, the rainbow that signifies your faithfulness, the flowers that show such beauty and the animals that reveal your comfort. Help us to be still, to allow ourselves to sit in the silence so we can hear you gentle voice. Help us to listen to our bodies when our body tells us to stop, take a nap, and be refreshed. O Lord, you know the value of rest. Help us to obey, and stop and rest. In Jesus' Name I pray. Amen.

Chapter 22

Generation To Generation

"For the Lord is good and his Love endures forever; his faithfulness continues through all generations" (Psalm 100:5 NIV).

"Hear O Israel: 'The Lord our God, the Lord is one. Love the Lord your God with all your heart and with all your soul and with all your strength. These commandments that I give you today are to be upon your hearts. Impress them on your children'" (Deuteronomy 6:4-6 NIV).

"You shall put these words of mine in your heart and soul, and you shall bind them as a sign on your hand, and fix the as an emblem on your forehead. Teach them to your children, talking about them when you are at home and when you are away, when you lie down and when you rise. Write them on the doorposts of your house" (Deuteronomy 11:18-20).

There are no words to express the magnitude of love felt for our children and grandchildren. To see the extension of self in them is overpowering. When the nurse brought our daughters, Diane, Kathy, and Christine, to me, when they were born, I was overwhelmed. They were God's beautiful creations. Then when my grandson was born, I remember putting my hand through the incubator to touch my premature 2lbs. 14 oz. grandson and feel our connection. He was so small that his father could put his son's hand through his wedding band. He graduated from University of Michigan majoring in anthropology and film documentary, and is getting his masters.

Our children can experience the world and we are so thankful for their sincere interest. My oldest granddaughter, Caitlin just returned from serving in the Peace Corps after three years in Mozambique, Africa. She was teaching English, living on a college campus and promoting soccer through acquired grants. She is now working for Soccer without Borders in Boston.

Another granddaughter, Kristin, graduated from Ohio University in communications and now works as an event planner. My third granddaughter, Lindsay, is studying at Michigan State with a major in Linguistics studies in the Arts and Humanities and minor in Global Studies.

I mention my grandchildren, of course, because I am so thrilled with all of their accomplishments, but also to give parents encouragement who are going through changes, divorce, and heartache. They remind me that our children are resilient and can come through these challenges and conflicts. Our family has experienced divorce, illnesses, death, and disruptions but have survived with much prayer.

One Sunday, I went to church with my daughter and her husband. A member of the church shared this story: When his son was two and a half years old many years ago, they took him to a restaurant. At the restaurant the child stood up in his high chair and announced loudly to the entire room to be quiet for they were going to pray. Everyone, including the waitresses stopped, got quiet and the just over two-year-old son, under no pressure, prayed. People told him afterward how nice that was for them.

A little child shall lead them we are told and we never know the influence we make in their lives as we instill God's ways and promises. Be encouraged to ask your children and grandchildren of their faith as they mature. For we want them to experience God's love, grace, forgiveness, mercy, and peace.

We are instructed to pray for them, to be encouragers, to remind them to whom they belong. So keep praying, be persistent, trusting and faithful in prayer to our living God. Keep holding on to Proverbs 22:6, which says, "Train your children in the right way, and when old, they will not stray."

O Lord, come, be with our children, our grandchildren, our families and help them and us to see you, to follow you. Please help them to seek your will for their lives. Help them find spouses that love you, will respect them and each other, and worship you. Help them discover you are *intertwined with them*, loving, holding, guiding and directing them. In Jesus' Name, Amen.

Chapter 23

Heaven On Earth - Now

"Thy kingdom come, Thy will be done on earth as it is in heaven." *Thy kingdom dwells in you*. I ask you to sit quietly and reflect on the above thought.

We have to begin to realize that God is living in us, God dwells within us, for we are God's dwelling place.

Nouwen tells us that we don't have to wait till we get to heaven to experience heaven on earth for it is within us. Jesus says, "Dwell in me as I dwell in you" (John 14:17 RSV) for it is this divine indwelling that is eternal life. Nouwen continues to say, "It is the active presence of God at the center of my living - the movement of God's Spirit within us - that gives us the eternal life."

"Holiness," says Carretto, "is nothing more than God dwelling within you and the conscious acceptance of being the dwelling place of God."

"Whatever it takes, live today as though God's dwelling with you is the clearest reality you have. Most Christians believe that intellectually without being conscious of it in their heart. Faith in this truth will cause you to see life through new lenses and will make his presence manifest. Know in your heart: God lives with you and in you." (*Daily Strength*, Strong Tower Christian Media)

From *Jesus Calling*: "Heaven is both present and future. As you walk along your life-path holding My hand, you are already in touch with the essence of heaven: nearness to Me. You can also find many hints of heaven along your pathway, because the earth is radiantly alive with My presence."

Pray: Oh Lord, this is again so real. You are so part of our lives, *intertwined*, dwelling within us. Help us realize we are forever bound, that you are with us through it all, the good and the difficulties of life, the thoughts that plague, the joys that surround. Help us take a breath – breathe - and relax in your Holy Spirit that will guide, direct, convict, correct, and comfort us. In Jesus' precious Name, Amen.

Chapter 24

We Are All Intertwined

Oh, my, a revelation, we are all intertwined, we are all one. Jesus tells us in:

John 17: 11b, "Holy Father, keep in Your name, them whom you have given Me, that they may be one as We [are one) (Amplified Bible).

In John 17:22-23, "I have given to them the glory and honor which You have given Me, that they may be one, [even] as We are one. I in them, You in Me, in order that they may become one and perfectly united" (Amplified Bible).

"I will continue to make [You] known, that the love which You have bestowed upon Me may be in them — felt in their hearts — and that I [Myself] may be in them" (John 17: 26b Amplified Bible).

We hear the cry for unity, for unity of those who believe in Jesus Christ to be united as one in and through the love of our Lord. Then we hear the cries, "How can we be one, when there are so many fractions of divisions?" We pray, from the Lord's Prayer ... "on earth as it is in heaven." Take a step back, a step forward, take a breath, is there division in heaven? "There is neither Jew nor Greek, slave nor free, male, nor female, for you are all one in Christ Jesus" (Galatians 3:28 NIV). We are one in the Spirit; we are one in the Lord. Praise God! What an awesome thought! Picture in your mind: *"all intertwined with Jesus."*

"The goal is for all of them to become one heart and mind — Just as you, Father, are in me and I in you. So they might be one heart and mind with us. Then the world might believe that you, in fact, sent me. The same glory you gave me, I gave them, so they'll be as unified and together as we are — I in them and you in me. Then they'll be mature in this oneness, and give the godless world evidence that you've sent me and loved them in the same way you've loved me" John 17 (*The Message Bible*).

Barclay in his *Daily Study Bible* shares that the prayer of Christ for the church in John 17 was: "that all its members would be one as He and his Father are one. The unity Jesus prayed for was a unity of personal relationship. A unity in which people loved each other because they loved Him, a unity based entirely on the relationship between heart and heart." He says, "Christians will never organize their churches all in the same way. They will never even all believe precisely the same things. But Christian unity transcends all these differences and joins people together in love. The cause of Christian unity at the present time and indeed all through history, has been injured and hindered, because people loved their own religious organizations, their own creeds, their own ritual, more than they loved each other. If we really loved each other and really loved Christ, no church would exclude anyone who was Christ's disciple. Only love implanted in our hearts by God can tear down the barriers which we have erected between one another and between our churches."

Pause, pray, meditate and express your own prayer.

Chapter 25

Reaching Out In Love

We are followers of Jesus all *intertwined in Jesus*. We are called to reach out to one another and to our neighbors showing love. God created the church so we could, "Be the church" bringing Jesus alive to all. So we can be encouragers, who were made whole and free and empowered to reach out in love.

It is so important to be in a church family. As we worship, share, celebrate, mourn, and support one another we become "family." I pray that your church has or is becoming your church family. Within this church family God has given each of us gifts and each person's gift is important for equipping God's church.

"Now here is what I am trying to say: all of you together are the one body of Christ and each one of you is a separate and necessary part of it. Here is a list of some of the parts he has placed in His church, which is His body: Apostles, Prophets – those who preach God's Word, Teachers, Those who do miracles, Those who have the gift of healing, Those who can help others, Those who can get others to work together, Those who speak in languages they have never learned" (1 Corinthians 12: 27-28, *The Living New Testament*).

"You are Christ's body-that's who you are! You must never forget this. Only as you accept your part of that body does your "part" mean anything" (1 Corinthians 12, *The Message Bible*).

Have you identified your gift that has been instilled within you? Do you know God's gift for you to use? You are an important member of God's church and God has asked you to use your gift and talent, and not bury it. And of all the gifts, the most important is love. If we don't love others and share our love, our gifts are nothing.

Pray: O Jesus, I am *intertwined with you* and I need your help and that of the Holy Spirit to show love to those you put on my path. Help me to see you within each person. For love is patient and kind. Love is not jealous or boastful. It is not arrogant or rude. Love does not insist on its own way. It is not irritable or resentful. It does not rejoice at wrong, but rejoices in the right. Love bears all things, believes all things, hopes all things, endures all things. Love never ends (1 Corinthians 13:4-8 RSV). Grant me patience to be your loving beloved as I live *intertwined in you*. Give me eyes and heart to reach out and love one another using the gifts you have given to me. In your Name I pray. Amen.

Chapter 26

Celebrate

I always loved the song, "Celebrate.", for it brings a smile to my face and I want to dance! A few words are: "Celebrate good times, come on! Bring your good times, we're going to celebrate." Let's celebrate God's goodness: Put the music on, start dancing, smile, God is with you, celebrate, come on.

Jesus entered the world in jubilation: "I am bringing you good news of great joy for all the people (Luke 2:10). Foster says, "Freedom from anxiety and care forms the basis of celebration. Because we know he cares for us we can cast our care upon him. God has turned our mourning into dancing…. Celebration brings, joy into life, and joy makes us strong."

Eldredge says, "To be fair, joy isn't exactly falling from the sky these days. We don't go out to gather it like manna. It's hard to come by…. We don't like to think about it much because it hurts to allow ourselves to feel how much we long for joy and how seldom it drops by. But joy is the point. I know it is. God says that joy is our strength. "The joy of the Lord is your strength" (Nehemiah. 8:l)… I can see that when I have felt joy, I have felt more alive than at any other time in my life."

Nouwen tells us, "The opposite of resentment is gratitude. Gratitude is at the heart of celebration and ministry. Gratitude is the attitude that enables us to let go of anger, receive the hidden gifts of those we want to serve and make these gifts visible to community as a source of celebration."

We are *intertwined with Jesus* never to be separated from our Jesus. We are linked and enfolded with our Jesus. Does this not bring you peace, blessed assurance and hope? Dance with your spouse, your friend, your sons and daughters, it's time to celebrate our inter-relationship with our Lord, our kinship, our oneness.

Did you forget that joy is one of the gifts of the spirit? (Galatians 5:22). It is our Lord's gift and acts (as Foster describes) as our motor that keeps everything else going. For joy produces energy and makes us strong.

"I have told you this so that my joy may be in you and your joy may be complete. As the Father has loved me, so I have loved you; abide in my love. If you keep my commandments, you will abide in my love, just as I have kept my Father's commandments and abide in his love" (John 15:9-11). "Joy comes from a consistent relationship with Jesus Christ. When our lives are *intertwined* with his, he will help us walk through adversity." (*Life Application Bible NRSV*)

As the hymn goes: "Trust and obey for there is no other way to be happy in Jesus but to trust and obey." For "blessed are those who hear the word of God and keep it" (Luke 11:28).

Foster cites Hannah Whitehall Smith's book, *The Christian's Secret of a Happy Life,* "to be the joy of obedience. Joy comes through obedience to Christ and joy results from obedience to Christ. Without obedience joy is hollow and artificial."

"A cheerful heart is good medicine" (Proverbs 17:22). Laughter is good for the soul. Laugh, get the cool whip out and put a little on your child's nose or cheek. Laugh. A memory I have of laughter is when I wore two different shoes to work one day. That day I was helping a child walk with his walker and he looked down and saw my shoes and just started laughing. Oh it was so much fun. One of the ladies at work asked if I was going home to change my shoes. I replied that I was having too much fun and would keep on laughing throughout the day. Laugh a big belly laugh and enjoy life.

Paul says: "Celebrate God all day, every day. I mean, revel in him! Make it as clear as you can to all you meet that you're on their side, working with them and not against them. Help them see that the Master is about to arrive. Don't fret or worry, instead of worrying, pray. Let petitions and praises shaped your worries into prayers, letting God know your concerns. Before you know it, a sense of God's wholeness, everything coming together for good, will come and settle you down. It's wonderful what happens when Christ displaces worry at the center of your life" (Philippians 4: 5-8 *The Message Bible*).

"Praise the Lord! Sing to the Lord a new song, his praise in the assembly of the faithful... Praise the Lord! Praise the Lord from the heavens; praise him in the heights! Praise him, all his angels; praise him, all his host! Let everything that breathes praise the Lord! Praise the Lord (Psalm 149, 148,150)!

Pray: O Lord we sing your praises! Lord Jesus we are so thankful. We are overjoyed and in gratitude for your great mercy, love, forgiveness and grace. In Jesus' Name we pray. Amen.

Chapter 27

Share and Tell

We just celebrated God's forgiveness, grace, mercy, and love for us. We danced and sang, so thankful for all that Christ has done for us. Jesus was with us, *intertwined*, and brought us through our difficult times.

Now we can't keep silent or the stones will cry out. We are to share God's goodness and faithfulness and promises with others. Jesus proclaimed his mission to be: "The spirit of the Lord God is upon me; ...He has sent me to bring good news to the oppressed, to bind up the brokenhearted, to proclaim liberty to the captives, and release to the prisoners. To proclaim the year of the Lord's favor and the day of vengeance of our God, to comfort all who mourn in Zion - to give them garland instead of ashes, the oil of gladness instead of mourning, the mantle of praise instead of a faint spirit"(Isaiah 61:1-3).

Recall and give thanks: God was present when I

_____.

God has helped or is helping me overcome

_____.

God forgave me: _____.

God _____.

As a *branch*, through Christ, our vine, we are *to bring forth fruit*. Murray says, "And so the believer needs to know that he is partaker of the divine nature, and has the very nature and spirit of Christ in him, and that his one calling is to yield himself to a perfect conformity to Christ." We are to remember that the branch (us) is in total dependence on the Vine (Christ) and has no cares. The Vine provides all of our needs and gives the strength to do all things."

The fruit of the (Holy) Spirit is, [the work that His presence within accomplishes] – is love, joy (gladness), peace, patience (an even temper, forbearance), kindness, goodness, faithfulness; (meekness, humility) gentleness, self-control (self-restraint) (Galatians 5:22-23 *Amplfied*).

We ask the Holy Spirit to work within us cultivating our *inner* fruits so that we can do the *outer* work that is presented before us. The outer work is the good work that each of us sees before us that we are called to do. Whether it is visiting the sick, or those in prison, leading Bible studies, preaching, working at a shelter, we are to use the gifts God has given us. "For I can do all things through Christ who strengthens me, but apart, we can do nothing" (Philippians 4:13, John 15:5).

Paul tells us, "Put on then, as God's chosen ones, holy and beloved, compassion, kindness, lowliness, meekness, and patience, forbearing one another and if one has a complaint against another, forgiving each other; as the Lord has forgiven you, so you also must forgive. And above all these put on love, which binds everything together in perfect harmony" (Colossians 3:12-14, *Revised Standard*).

We are responsible for choosing to live as Christ would want us to live. As our Lord works in us to produce these fruits, we can *share* God's goodness as we *tell* others of God's great love for us and what God has done. "For God did not give us a spirit of timidity but a spirit of power and love and of self-control" (2 Timothy 1:7 RSV).

So go forth boldly in the power of the Holy Spirit for Jesus lives within you, *intertwined!* Praise the Lord.

Pray: O Lord, create in me a clean heart. Help me to put on and develop the spiritual gifts within me. Then show me how you want me to serve others using the gifts that you have given me. Empower and equip me to tell others of your great love and what you have done in me. Help me not to be silent. Help me to boldly speak in simple terms and share your great love, so others can experience your forgiveness, mercy, grace, and love, and become *intertwined in Jesus.* In Jesus' Name I pray, Amen.

Chapter 28

Peace

"The Lord is my shepherd (to feed, guide and shield me); I shall not lack. He makes me lie down in (fresh, tender) green pastures; He leads me beside the still and restful waters. He refreshes and restores my life – my self; He leads me in the paths of righteousness (uprightness and right standing with Him – not for my earning it, but) for His name's sake. Yes, though I walk through the (deep sunless) valley of the shadow of death, I will fear or dread no evil; for You are with me; Your rod (to protect) and Your staff (to guide), they comfort me. You prepare a table before me in the presence of my enemies; You anoint my head with oil; my (brimming) cup runs over. Surely (or only) goodness, mercy and unfailing love shall follow me all the days of my life; and through the length of days the house of the Lord (and His presence) shall be my dwelling place" (Psalm 23, Amplified Bible).

At 56 years of age, I was called to enter the seminary. One morning as I was driving to Bethany Theological Seminary, I was so very nervous for I was taking my first theology test. I stopped at a gas station to get gas. As I went to pay at the gas station, I encountered a woman with the most radiant illuminating smile. This lady had no idea the impact she was having on my life at that moment for it brought peace to my soul. I will hold the essence of this smile within me forever. We don't always know how we affect one another as God's light shines and brings us God's peace.

I would like to invite you now to sit back and contemplate the question, "What brings you peace?" Take a breath; breathe out all problems, distractions, hurts, confusion, agitations right now. Allow God's peace to surround you, to enfold you, to come upon you, and rest in this position. I invite you to be still, no words needed, just remain quiet and enjoy God's presence and peace. Stay as long as you wish.

"And God's peace (be yours, that tranquil state of a soul assured of its salvation through Christ, and so fearing nothing from God and content with its earthly lot of whatever sort that is, that peace) which transcends all understanding, shall garrison and mount guard over your hearts and minds in Christ Jesus"(Philippians 4:7 Amplified).

And God's peace which passes all understanding will be yours. "And God's peace that passes all understanding... "Say it over and over sitting quietly, resting in God's peace. Be still, assured of your salvation, knowing the Lord is with you, and is embracing you. Imagine Jesus' arms around you, and peace penetrating your very soul, your inner being. Let this come upon you as you rest in the love of Jesus.

Jesus tells us: "Peace I leave with you; my peace I give to you. I do not give to you as the world gives. Do not let your hearts be troubled and do not let them be afraid" (John 14:27).

"Peace is my continual gift to you. It flows abundantly from My throne of grace. Just as the Israelites could not store up manna for the future but had to gather it daily, so it is with My Peace. The day — by — day collecting of manna kept my people aware of their dependence on Me. Similarly, I give you sufficient Peace for the present, when you come to me by prayer and petition with thanksgiving… I have designed you to need Me moment by moment. As your awareness of your neediness increases, so does your realization of My abundant sufficiency. I can meet every one of your needs without draining my resources at all. Approach my throne of grace with bold confidence, receiving My Peace with a thankful heart" (*Jesus Calling*).

As you realize this, Carretto says, "Nothing will ever be able to make you afraid again since you carry God Himself and His omnipotence within yourselves. You will have peace because peace is fruit of the order I have established between heaven (which is God) and earth (which is you)."

"And I will dwell in the presence of the Lord forever." And I am, and will be *intertwined with Jesus* forever. Oh, we just can't imagine. "No eye has seen, no ear has heard, no mind has conceived what God has prepared for those who love him" (1 Corinthians 2:9 NIV).

You and I will experience the peace that passes understanding completely. We will be whole. Jesus tells us that we can be assured that "Jesus will come again and will take you to myself so that where I am, you may be also" (John 14:3).

"Now to him who is able to keep you from falling, and to present you without blemish before the presence of his glory with rejoicing, to the only God our Savior, through Jesus Christ our Lord, be glory, majesty, power, authority, before all time and now and forever"(Jude:24 *RSV*).

"The Lord bless you and keep you; the Lord make his face to shine upon you, and be gracious to you; the Lord lift up his countenance upon you, and give you peace" (Numbers 6:24-26). In Jesus' Name. Amen.

Chapter 29

Poem: Only A Branch

Only A Branch
by Freda Hanbury

'Tis only a little Branch, A thing so fragile and weak,
But that little Branch hath a message true
To give, could it only speak.

"I'm only a little Branch,
I live by a life not mine,
For the sap that flows through my tendrils small
Is the life-blood of the Vine.

"No power indeed have I
The fruit of myself to bear,
But since I'm part of the living Vine,
Its fruitfulness I share.

"Dost thou ask how I abide?
How this life I can maintain?—
I am bound to the Vine by life's strong band,
And I only need remain.

"Where first my life was given,
In the spot where I am set,
Upborne and upheld as the days go by,
By the stem which bears me yet.

"I fear not the days to come,
I dwell not upon the past,
As moment by moment I draw a life,
Which for evermore shall last.

"I bask in the sun's bright beams,
Which with sweetness fills my fruit,
Yet I own not the clusters hanging there,
For they all come from the root."

A life which is not my own,
But another's life in me:
This, this is the message the Branch would speak,
A message to thee and me.

Oh, struggle not to "abide,"
Nor labor to bring forth fruit,"
But let Jesus unite thee to Himself,
As the Vine Branch to the root.

So simple, so deep, so strong
That union with Him shall be:
His life shall forever replace thine own,
And His love shall flow through thee.

For His Spirit's fruit is love,
And love shall thy life become,
And for evermore on His heart of love
Thy Spirit shall have her home.

Endnotes

Introduction:

Upper Room, Where the world meets to Pray,
Stephen D. Bryant, (Upper Room,
Nashville, TN), July 7, 2017.
Intertwined Beverly and Barbara in the Womb,
Beverly Beeghly Avers, (Fairway Press),
2014.
The Practice of the Presence of God,
Brother Lawrence, (Barbour Publishing,
Inc.), Uhrichsvile, Ohio, 2004.

Chapter 1: Meaning Of *Intertwined*

Jesus Calling, Sarah Young, (Thomas Nelson),
Nashville, TN 2004. Dec. 30, Oct. 23.

Chapter 2: John 15:1-5, Vine and the Branches

The True Vine, Andrew Murray, Moody Publisher,
Chicago, IL, 1983. pp.16, 43, 9, 44.

Chapter 3: Daily Appointment With God

My Utmost for His Highest, Oswald Chambers,
edited by James Reimann, (Discovery
House Publishers), Uhrichsville, OH, 1992.
Jesus Lives, Sarah Young, (Thomas Nelson),
Nashville, TN, 2009.
Daily Strength, (Strong Tower Christian Media),
Walk thru the Bible Ministries, Inc., 2018.

The Beloved Disciple, Beth Moore, (Broadman & Holman Publishers), Nashville, TN, 2003, pp.38,41.

The Heart of Henri Nouwen (His Words of Blessing), Rebecca Laird and Michael J. Christensen, (Crossroad Publishing Co.), 2003. pp. 113-114, 13, 23, 26.

The Meaning of Prayer, Harry Emerson Fosdick, Association Press, 1949. p. 30.

If You Will Ask (Reflections on the Power of Prayer), Oswald Chambers, (Discovery House Publishers), Uhrichsville, OH, 1937, p. 14.

The Awakened Heart, (Opening Yourself to The Love you Need, Gerald G. May, M.D. (HarperCollins Publishers), New York, NY, 1991, p. 164.

Chapter 4: First And Greatest Commandment

Henri Nouwen, Spiritual Formation (Following the Movements of the Spirit) with Michael J. Christensen and Rebecca J. Laird, (HarperCollins), New York, N.Y. p. XV11.

The Heart of Henri Nouwen (His Words of Blessing), Rebecca Laird and Michael J. (Christensen, Crossroad Publishing Co.) 2003. pp, 17-19.

A Testament of Devotion, Thomas R. Kelly, (Harper & Brothers Publishers), New York, 1941, p. 29.

Care of the Soul (A guide for cultivating depth and sacredness in everyday life), Thomas Moore, (HarperCollins Publishers), 1992, pp. 4, 5.

Chapter 5: Falling In Love

The True Vine, Andrew Murray. Moody Publisher,
Chicago, IL, 1983, pp. 17, 41, 43, 44-45, 127.

Chapter 6: Worship, Communion, Praise

Introduction to Christian Worship (Revised Edition),
James White, Abington Press, Nashville,
1980, p. 26
Christian Worship, James F. White, (Abingdon
Press), Nashville, 1980, pp. 26, 29, 35.
*Henri Nouwen, Spiritual Formation (Following the
Movements of the Spirit)* with Michael J.
Christensen and Rebecca J. Laird,
(HarperCollins), New York, N.Y. p. 64.
Daily Strength,(Strong Tower Christian Media),
Walk thru the Bible Ministries, Inc.,
7/25/2018

Chapter 7: I Am Of Worth

The Heart of Henri Nouwen (His Words of Blessing),
Rebecca Laird and Michael J. Christensen,
(Crossroad Publishing Co.), 2003, p. 33.
*Henri Nouwen, Spiritual Formation (Following the
Movements of the Spirit)* with Michael J.
Christensen and Rebecca J. Laird,
(HarperCollins), New York, NY, p. 81.
The God Who Comes, Carlo Carretto, (Orbis Books),
Maryknoll, New York, 1997. p. 89, 17.
You are Beloved, Rev. Bobby Schuller, Hour
of Power.com, Creed.

Daily Strength, (Strong Tower Christian Media),
    Walk thru the Bible Ministries, Inc.,
    9/18/2017.

Chapter 8: Our Power: Holy Spirit

If You Will Ask (Reflections on the Power of Prayer)
    Oswald Chambers, (Discovery House
    Publishers), Uhrichsville, OH, 1937. pp. 116.
A Shepherd Looks at Psalm 23, W. Phillip Keller,
    (Zondervan.com), Grand Rapids, Michigan,
    2007, p. 122.
The Spiritual Life, Evelyn Underhill, (Morehouse
    Publishing), New York, NY, 1995 p. 32.
If You Will Ask (Reflections on the Power of Prayer)
    Oswald Chambers, (Discovery House
    Publishers), Uhrichsville, Ohio, 1937.
    pp. 110,113.
My Utmost for His Highest, Oswald Chambers,
    edited by James Reimann, (Discovery
    House Publishers), Uhrichsville, OH, 1992,
    Sept. 4, Jan. 23.

Chapter 9: Do It Now

A Testament of Devotion, Thomas R. Kelly, (Harper
    & Brothers Publishers), New York, 1941.
    pp. 38-39,116, 120, 43, 95-96, 124.
Walking with God (Talk to Him: Hear From Him.
    Really) John Eldredge, (Thomas Nelson),
    2008, p. 149.
*Henri Nouwen, Spiritual Formation (Following the
    Movements of the Spirit)* with Michael J.
    Christensen and Rebecca J. Laird,

(HarperCollins, New York, NY), p. 27.

Chapter 10: Discipline

Walking with God (Talk to Him: Hear From Him.
Really) John Eldredge, (Thomas Nelson),
2008, p. 17.

*Henri Nouwen, Spiritual Formation (Following the
Movements of the Spirit)* with Michael J.
Christensen and Rebecca J. Laird,
(HarperCollins), New York, NY, pp. 18, 28.

The Heart of Henri Nouwen (His Words of Blessing),
Rebecca Laird and Michael J. Christensen,
(Crossroad Publishing Co.), 2003,
pp. 99-100,xv11.

My Utmost for His Highest, Oswald Chambers,
edited by James Reimann, (Discovery
House Publishers), Uhrichsville, OH, 1992,
July 2.

*Celebration of Discipline (The Path to Spiritual
Growth)*, Richard J. Foster, (Harper & Row,
Publishers), New York, 1978, p. 2, 9.2.

The Gospel of John Volume Two, William Barclay,
(Westminister John Knox Press), Louisville,
KY, 2001, p. 205.

Illustrations Unlimited, James S. Hewett, editor,
(Tyndale House Publisher, Inc.), Wheaton,
Illinois, 1988, p. 417.

Chapter 11: Inter-Twin-Ed With Jesus

Intertwined Beverly and Barbara in the Womb,
Beverly Beeghly Avers,(Fairway Press),
2014.

Jesus Calling, Sarah Young, (Thomas Nelson), Nashville, TN, 2004. November 13.

Chapter 12: The Mind

Battlefield of the Mind, Winning the Battle in Your Mind, Joyce Meyer. (FaithWords), Hachette Book Group, New York, NY.1995, pp. 60, 61, 64, 41, 169.

Walking with God (Talk to Him: Hear From Him. Really) John Eldredge, (Thomas Nelson), 2008, p. 39.

Jesus Lives, Sarah Young, (Thomas Nelson), Nashville, TN, 2009, p. 80.

Celebration of Discipline (The Path to Spiritual Growth) Richard J. Foster, (Harper & Row Publishers), New York, 1978, p.167.

Chapter 13: The Pit

A Shepherd Looks at Psalm 23, W. Phillip Keller, (Zondervan.com), Grand Rapids, Michigan, 2007, pp. 70, 75, 41.

Jesus Lives, Sarah Young, (Thomas Nelson), Nashville, TN, 2009, p. 28-29.

Chapter 14: Suicide

The Red Sea Rules, Robert J. Morgan, (W. Publishing Group, Thomas Nelson), Nashville, Tennessee, 2014, Preface.

Chapter 15: Loving Oneself

> *Jesus Calling*, Sarah Young, (Thomas Nelson),
> Nashville, TN 2004, July 18.

Chapter 16: Divorce

> *Jesus Lives*, Sarah Young, (Thomas Nelson),
> Nashville, TN, 2009. p.186.
> *Daily Strength*, (Strong Tower Christian Media),
> Walk thru the Bible Ministries, Inc., 2018,
> Sept. 18, 2017.

Chapter 17: Grief

> *Jesus Lives*, Sarah Young, (Thomas Nelson),
> Nashville, Tenn., 2009, p. 32.
> *Henri Nouwen, Spiritual Formation (Following the
> Movements of the Spirit)* with Michael J.
> Christensen and Rebecca J. Laird,
> (HarperCollins), New York, NY, pp. 43, 64.
> *Nearing Home, Life, Faith, and Finishing Well*, Billy
> Graham, (Thomas Nelson Inc.), Nashville,
> TN, 2011. pp. 100-106.
> *Intertwined Beverly & Barbara in the Womb*, Beverly
> Beeghly Avers, (Fairway Press), Fairway
> Press.Com, pp. 49-53.

Chapter 18: God Winks

> *When God Winks at You*, Squire Rushnell, (W
> Publishing Group, an imprint of Thomas
> Nelson), Nashville, Tennessee, 2006, pp. 3-4.

The Awakened Heart, (Opening Yourself to The Love you Need, Gerald G. May, M.D. (HarperCollins Publishers), New York, N.Y, 1991, p. 135.

Chapter 20: Pots And Pans And Diapers Too

Practice of the Presence of God, Brother Lawrence, (Barbour Publishing, Inc.), Uhrichsville, Ohio, 2004. pp. 26, 40.

Chapter 21: Rest

Jesus Lives, Sarah Young, (Thomas Nelson), Nashville, Tenn., 2009, p.266.
Walking with God (Talk to Him: Hear From Him. Really) John Eldredge, (Thomas Nelson), 2008, pgs.27-28.
Daily Strength, (Strong Tower Christian Media), Walk thru the Bible Ministries, Inc., Sabbath Rest, Take a break: LeAnne Martin, July, August, 2018.

Chapter 23: Heaven On Earth - Now

The Heart of Henri Nouwen (His Words of Blessing), Rebecca Laird and Michael J. Christensen, (Crossroad Publishing Co.), 2003, p. 187.
The God who Comes, Carlo Carretto,(Orbis Books), Maryknoll, New York, 1997. p. 224.
Daily Strength, (Strong Tower Christian Media), Walk thru the Bible Ministries, Inc., "Presence", 12/27/2017.

Jesus Calling, Sarah Young, (Thomas Nelson), Nashville, TN, 2004, April 14.

Chapter 24: We Are All Intertwined

William Barclay, The New Daily Study Bible, The Gospel of John Volume two, (Westminister John Knox Press), Louisville, KY, 2001, John 17, p. 254.

Chapter 26: Celebrate

Celebration, written by Bryan Adams, Ian Honeyman, Klaus Badet, 1980, Kool & the Gang, Warner-Chappel Music Inc., Old River Music and WB Music Corp.

Walking with God (Talk to Him: Hear From Him. Really) John Eldredge, (Thomas Nelson), 2008, p. 39.

Henri Nouwen, Spiritual Formation (Following the Movements of the Spirit) with Michael J. Christensen and Rebecca J. Laird, (HarperCollins), New York, NY, p. 63.

Celebration of Discipline (The Path to Spiritual Growth) Richard J. Foster, (Harper & Row Publishers), New York, 1978, pp.163-165.

Chapter 27: Share And Tell

The True Vine, Andrew Murray, Moody Publisher, Chicago, IL., 1983, pp. 16-17.

Chapter 28: Peace

Jesus Calling, Sarah Young, (Thomas Nelson),
Nashville, TN, 2004, April 18.
The God Who Comes, Carlo Carretto, (Orbis Books),
Maryknoll, New York, 1997, p. 225.